Passport's Illustrated Travel Guide to

GREEK ISLANDS

FROM
THOMAS
COOK

PASSPORT BOOKS
a division of *NTC Publishing Group*
Lincolnwood, Illinois USA

Published by Passport Books,
an imprint of NTC/Contemporary Publishing Company,
4255 W. Touhy Avenue,
Lincolnwood (Chicago), Illinois
60646–1975 U.S.A.

Written by Robin Gauldie

Original photography by Steve Day, Terry Harris, Rob
Moore, Anthony Sattin and James Tims

Edited, designed and produced by AA Publishing.
© The Automobile Association 1996.
Maps © The Automobile Association 1996.

Library of Congress Catalog Card Number: 95-73295

ISBN 0-8442-4830-4

The contents of this publication are believed correct at the time of
printing. Nevertheless, the publishers cannot accept responsibility for
any errors or omissions, or for changes in the details given in this guide,
or for the consequences of any reliance on the information provided by
the same. Assessments of attractions, hotels, restaurants, and so forth
are based upon the author's own experience, and therefore descriptions
given in this guide necessarily contain an element of subjective opinion
which may not reflect the publisher's opinion or dictate a reader's own
experiences on another occasion.
**We have tried to ensure accuracy in this guide, but things do
change and we would be grateful if readers would advise us of any
inaccuracies they may encounter.**

Published by Passport Books in conjunction with AA Publishing and the
Thomas Cook Group Ltd.

Color separation: BTB Colour Reproduction, Whitchurch, Hampshire,
England.

Printed by Edicoes ASA, Oporto, Portugal.

Second printing 1997.

Contents

About this Book

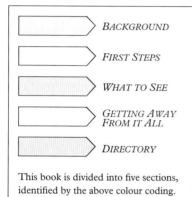

BACKGROUND

FIRST STEPS

WHAT TO SEE

GETTING AWAY
FROM IT ALL

DIRECTORY

This book is divided into five sections,
identified by the above colour coding.

Throughout the Greek Islands, tourism and the
old ways live side by side

Background gives an introduction to
the islands – their history, geography,
politics, culture.

First Steps offers practical advice on
arriving and getting around.

What to See is an alphabetical listing of
the places to visit, interspersed with
walks and tours.

Getting Away From it All highlights
places off the beaten track where it's
possible to relax and enjoy peace and
quiet.

Finally, the **Directory** provides
practical information – from shopping
and entertainment to children and
sport. Special highly illustrated features
on specific aspects of the islands appear
throughout the book.

BACKGROUND

'The isles of Greece, the isles of Greece!
Where burning Sappho loved and sung,
Where grew the arts of war and peace,
Where Dílos rose and Phoebus sprung,
    Eternal summer gilds them yet,
    But all, except their sun, is set.'
GEORGE GORDON, LORD BYRON
(1788–1824), *Don Juan*

Introduction

*V*ariety is the spice of the Greek islands. Some visitors go in search of the ancient and medieval worlds of temples, castles and fortresses. Others seek peaceful harbour or hill-top villages and secluded coves. Millions more are simply looking for a good time in bustling holiday resorts with sandy beaches, friendly tavernas and discos. All of these are waiting to be discovered.

Island life is lived at a slower pace than life in the streets of Athens and other mainland cities, and each island moves to its own rhythm, with its own traditions, landscape and architecture.

Through the long summer months, Greek islanders spend most of their time outdoors, though sensibly they avoid the fierce middle-of-the-day temperatures by staying indoors and taking a siesta, and during the afternoon many places resemble ghost towns.

For visitors, however, there is no better way to pass the hot afternoon than sitting at a shady harbourside table with a glass of cold beer or a carafe of retsina and a plate of prawns or octopus landed fresh that morning.

You can stay in the bright, newly-built apartments and hotels of the popular resorts, seek out smaller pensions or village rooms in quiet hideaways, or find comfortably-restored old homes, traditional shipowners' mansions, or secluded luxury hotels.

The Aegean and Ionian seas offer some of the best yachting and windsurfing in Europe, plus water-skiing, parascending, diving and snorkelling from dozens of sunny beaches.

FORMER YUGOSLAV REPUBLIC OF MACEDONIA

ALBANIA

Kérkyra

GREECE

Paxoí

Ionia

Lefkáda

Kefalloniá

Ithåki

Nisía

Ionian Sea

Zákynthos

Pelopónnisos

Mediterranean Sea

0   100   200 km

THE GREEK ISLANDS

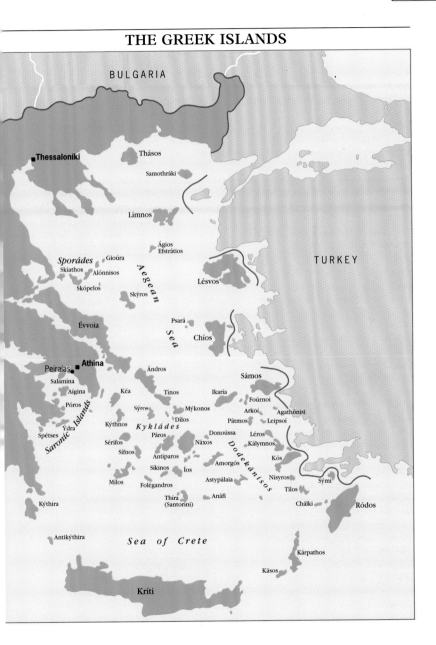

BULGARIA

■Thessaloníki

Thásos

Samothráki

Límnos

Ágios
Efstrátios

Sporádes Gioúra
Skíathos Alónnisos

Skópelos

Skýros

TURKEY

Lésvos

Aegean

Évvoia

Psará

Chíos

Sea

Peiraías ■Athína

Ándros

Sámos

Salamína

Aígina

Kéa

Tínos

Ikaría

Póros

Foúrnoi

Sýros

Mýkonos

Arkoí

Agathónisi

Ýdra

Kýthnos *Kykládes*

Dílos

Pátmos

Leipsoí

Spétses

Páros

Donoússa

Léros

Saronic Islands

Sérifos

Náxos

Kálymnos

Sífnos

Kós

Antíparos

Sikinos

Amorgós

Dodekánisos

Milos

Íos

Astypálaia

Nísyros

Sými

Folégandros

Tílos

Kýthira

Thíra
(Santoríni)

Anáfi

Chálki

Ródos

Antikýthira

Sea of Crete

Kárpathos

Kásos

Kríti

History

BC
3000
Seafaring Bronze Age trading culture
develops in Cyclades.
2200–1700
Early Minoan civilisation in Crete
develops into Minoan palace culture and
trade empire.
1600
Mycenaean culture spreads to islands
from Greek mainland.
c1470
Explosion of Thíra volcano. Collapse of
Minoan civilisation.
1200
Waning of Mycenaean culture.
c100
Arrival of Dorian Greeks in Aegean
islands.
800–600
City-state system takes shape.
490
First Persian invasion. Athenian victory
at Marathónas.
480
Second Persian invasion. Persian fleet
destroyed at Salamis.
479
Persian defeats on mainland end Persian
wars.
478
Athens dominates the islands as leader of
Delian league.
431–404
Peloponnesian War between Sparta and
Athens ending in Athenian defeat.
358–336
Rise of Macedonia.
336–323
Reign of Alexander the Great.
323–196
Era of Macedonian kings.

215–146
Wars with Rome, culminating in Roman
conquest.
1st century BC
Pompey clears pirates from Aegean
islands.
AD
260–8
Gothic fleets raid islands.
330
Roman Emperor Constantine moves his
capital to Byzantium (Istanbul),
renaming it Constantinople and founding
the Christian Byzantine empire in Greece
and the east.
600–900
Arab corsairs conquer Crete, sack
Rhodes and raid Aegean islands.
960–1
Byzantine general Nikiforos Fokas
recovers Crete.
1204
Frankish/Venetian Fourth Crusade sacks
Constantinople. Venetians take Crete,
the Ionian islands, and Evia. Knights of
St John take Rhodes, Kós and the
Dodecanese. Cyclades come under rule
of the Sanudo Dukes of Náxos, vassals of
the Frankish King of Athens. Genoa
acquires Northeast Aegean islands.
1354–1453
Turkish conquest of Byzantine Empire
culminates in fall of Constantinople.
1499–1530
Turks conquer Venetian strongholds on
mainland.
1522
Turks take Rhodes.
1566
Turks conquer Chíos and Náxos.
1571
Turks checked at sea-battle of Lepanto

by Holy League led by Don John of Austria, but in same year take Sámos.

1669
Turks capture Crete.

1797
Revolutionary France seizes Corfu and Ionian islands from Venice.

1814–64
British protectorate of Corfu and the Ionian.

1821–30
War of Independence. The Cyclades and the Argo-Saronic islands with parts of the mainland become the new Republic of Greece.

1831
President Capodistrias assassinated.

1833
Bavarian Prince Otto becomes King Otho I of the Hellenes.

1864
Britain cedes Corfu and Ionian islands to Greece.

1866
Cretan revolt against Turkey fails.

1912
First Balkan War. Greece annexes Chíos. Italy seizes Rhodes and the Dodecanese from Turkey.

1913
Second Balkan War. Cretan revolt succeeds. Crete joins Greece after brief independence. Many Cretan Muslims migrate to Rhodes. Greece annexes Lésvos, Sámos and Ikaría.

1917
Greece joins World War I on side of Britain, France and Italy.

1919
Encouraged by Britain and France, Greece lands troops at Smyrna (Izmir) in Turkey.

1920–3
War between Greece and Turkey ends in defeat for Greece. Around one million Greeks driven from Turkey.

1924–36
Political chaos, leading to suspension of constitution. General Metaxas becomes dictator.

1940
Battleship *Elli* sunk by Italian submarine. Italy demands access to mainland Greek ports. Metaxas refuses. Italian invasion defeated.

1941–4
German and Italian occupation of mainland and islands. Varied resistance groups active, especially on Crete. British commando raids on Dodecanese islands.

1946–9
Civil war on mainland, with the USA and Britain supporting the Royalist right wing government forces against the left.

1947
Rhodes and the Dodecanese join Greece.

1953
Earthquake.

1967–74
Military junta led by Colonel George Papadopoulos rules Greece. King Constantine expelled. Referendum ends the monarchy.

1974
Collapse of the junta after the Turkish invasion of Cyprus. Restoration of democracy.

1981
Greece joins the European Community. Left wing PASOK party led by Andreas Papandreou elected.

1985
PASOK re-elected.

1989
PASOK defeated. Series of short-lived caretaker governments.

1990
Nea Dimokratia party elected under Konstantinos Mitsotakis.

1993
PASOK re-elected.

Island Dwellers

The Cyclades in the Bronze Age
The first metal-using civilisation in Greece flourished in the Cyclades around 3000BC, leaving behind bronze tools and implements and remarkably modern-looking carvings.

The Minoans
For five centuries, from around 2000BC, the Minoan empire based on Crete was the greatest power in the Aegean, exacting tribute from mainland Greek princes and controlling colonies throughout the Cyclades.

The Mycenaeans and Dorians
As Minoan power waned the warlike bronze-using Mycenaeans (of Homer's sagas) expanded from the mainland into Crete and the Cyclades. From around 1100BC they were followed by the first Greek-speaking, iron-using Dorian settlers.

The classical era
In the city-state era many of the islands possessed powerful navies and merchant fleets and often vied with Athens for control of Greek seas. Several sided with Persia during the Persian Wars. At the height of its power Athens controlled the Delian League of island states (those surrounding the sacred island of Dílos) but many of the islands aligned themselves with Sparta against Athens during the Peloponnesian Wars.

Alexander and his heirs
With the rise of Macedon, the islands came under the sway of Alexander and his successors and the Ptolemies of Egypt used Thíra as a naval base.

The Romans
In 229BC Corfu and the Ionian group became the first Greek islands to fall to Rome. However, by the time Roman subjugation of Greece was completed, with the conquest of Athens in 86BC, many of the Aegean islands had become pirate havens and, in the first century BC, the Roman general Pompey built a fleet to clear the outlaws from the sea.

Rebellions against Turkish rule from the 16th to 20th centuries were bloodily suppressed

The Byzantine empire

The power of Constantinople waned in the seventh and eighth centuries and Arabs from Spain conquered Crete, sacked Rhodes and raided the Aegean islands. In AD960–1 the Byzantine general, Nikiforos Fokas, reconquered Crete, but by the 11th century the Normans of Sicily and the Venetians were raiding the Ionian islands.

Venetians, Genoese and Crusaders

Troops of the Italian Infantry Regiment invade Corfu in 1940

Venice, with its eye on the Greek islands, encouraged its Frankish allies of the Fourth Crusade to sack Constantinople in 1204. The Venetians then seized Évvoia (Evia), the Ionian islands, Crete, and bases on the mainland. The Cyclades became the Duchy of Náxos, ruled by the Venetian Sanudo family, and the Dodecanese were taken by the Knights of the Order of St John, who also fortified Rhodes and Kós. Genoa acquired the Northeast Aegean islands through the marriage of a Genoese prince to a Byzantine princess.

The Turks in the Greek Islands

The Turkish conquest of mainland Greece, except for a few Venetian strongholds, was complete by 1460 but the islands held out for much longer. Crete did not fall until 1669 and Tínos held out until 1715. Corfu was threatened, but remained part of the Venetian empire until conquered by France in 1797. Turkish rule was a mixture of brutality and negligence.

Many seafarers grew rich on the sea-trade of the Ottoman Empire (which the Greeks controlled) but islanders who rebelled against the Sultan were massacred.

The British in the Ionian

Britain ousted the French from Corfu in 1814 and the seven Ionian islands remained in British hands until 1864 when they were handed back to Greece.

The Italians in the Dodecanese

Italy seized the Dodecanese from Turkey in 1912, making Rhodes the provincial capital and Léros the eastern base of the Italian navy. The Italians restored the Palace of the Grand Masters and the fortifications of Rhodes and left behind many ornate public buildings. When Italy surrendered in 1943 its Aegean possessions were occupied by the Germans and there were destructive raids by British commandos. In 1947 the Dodecanese at last became part of Greece.

Geography

*G*reece claims some 2,000 islands, islets, rocks and skerries, from Corfu off the northwest coast to Rhodes (and just beyond) in the southeast. Six of these, Corfu and its satellites, are in the Ionian Sea, a southern extension of the Adriatic. The rest clutter the Aegean Sea, with Crete separating them from the Eastern Mediterranean. Some are just a stone's throw from foreign shores: Corfu is separated by little more than a kilometre of water from Albania, and tiny Megísti (Kastellórizon) is only 500m from the Turkish coast. Many are mountainous and barren, others are well-watered and fertile, and the tremendous variety of island landscapes is part of their never-ending charm.

Climate
Each island has its own microclimate, influenced by the sea, prevailing winds and nearby landmasses. Spring comes earliest to Crete, which has the hottest summers too. Rhodes has more hours of sunshine than any other island, while Corfu and the Ionian isles have slightly milder summers. The Cyclades are swept by the gale-force *meltemi*, which can blow for up to three days at a time in summer. Sámos and the Northeast Aegean islands, close to the Turkish coast, have late springs, influenced by the snowy heights of the Anatolian plateau. From late May to October rain is rare.

Economy and population
About 1.3 million Greeks are islanders, living on 169 inhabited islands. Many of these have only a handful of natives, like tiny Maratho with just five people, whereas Crete is home to more than half a million. Tourism is a big employer on many islands, but fishing and farming are still important. Quarrying for marble and pumice is also a contributor to several island economies, and money sent home by Greeks living overseas helps many families to manage.

Farming
Oranges, lemons, vines and, above all, olives grow abundantly on the more fertile islands. On smaller, drier isles barley and wheat grow on terraces and goats graze on higher ground. Age-old implements and practices are only now being replaced by modern tools and methods on remoter islands.

Fishing
Island fishermen seek squid, sardines, mackerel, red mullet and other prizes. The Aegean has been fished intensively for millennia and catches are getting

Greek island landscapes range from sulphurous volcanic craters to peaceful green valleys

Deep natural harbours on many islands have helped to shape Greece as a maritime nation

smaller, but demand is high and prices for seafood are pushed higher by tourism.

Flora and fauna

Many of the islands are rewarding for snorkellers and birdwatchers and a rich insect and reptile fauna includes species found nowhere else in Europe. Rare sea turtles nest on some island beaches (see pages 42–3). Wildflowers provide a blaze of spring colour.

Geology

The porous limestone rock of many islands allows rainfall to soak quickly away. Others, like Sámos, Samothráki or Ikaría are granite outcrops. Santoríni's unique landscapes are the result of millennia of vulcanism, and Nísyros too has a slumbering volcanic crater. Marble is quarried on Páros and Thásos, and quarries on Mílos and Thíra (Santoríni) produce cement.

The sea

In ancient times the sea linked the islands with the empires of the Middle East. In the 15th and 16th centuries the sea spelt prosperity for some but peril for others from pirate raids. Greek island captains controlled the wealthy trade of the Ottoman Empire, and in the War of Independence turned their guns on the Turks. The sea also unites the scattered islands and provides a living for thousands of sailors and fishermen. Small sailing brigs (caïques) were the trade lifeline for many islands well into the 20th century and every island has its quota of old salts from the Greek merchant navy.

The sea also provided an emigration route for islanders, most of them heading to the USA, Australia, Canada and South Africa though many of them bring their families 'home' for a summer visit.

Culture

Living traditions

Visitors to the islands may still see grain being winnowed on a stone threshing-floor and bread being baked in a wood-fired oven. Mules and donkeys are still vital load-carriers for farmers on steep hillsides. These days, though, the grain will not have been ground in an island mill. The surviving windmills in places like Mýkonos have become chic holiday homes, and flour for the bakeries comes from big mills on the mainland.

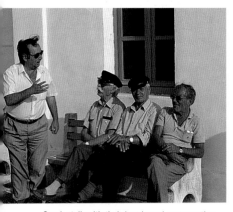

Greeks talk with their hands and conversation is always animated

Boats and planes

Big, fast, modern ferries, high-speed hydrofoils and jet aircraft have taken the place of the caïques and steamers of the old days, bringing the islands closer to the mainland and the outside world. Islands with international airports or domestic flights to Athens are the envy of those without, and charter flights are seen by every islander as the key to a fast tourism fortune.

The tourism boom

Charter flights now go straight to a dozen holiday isles from the big cities of Europe, bringing up to 8 million tourists a year to the beaches of their dreams. Islanders who once scraped a bare living from handkerchief-sized fields and thorny goat pasture now grow prosperous from holidaymakers; jobs are created, and there is far more incentive for young islanders to stay at home, instead of seeking a livelihood on the mainland or overseas. Moribund villages have been reborn and tottering houses rebuilt.

Change for the better?

Have all the changes been positive? Most definitely not. Once-tranquil havens are lined with noisy bars and discos, unsilenced motorbikes boom down narrow streets, and thriving resorts have mushroomed on unspoiled island beaches. The tourism season is mostly summer only, and competition for tourist drachmas in peak season can be intense and unseemly.

That said, the islands remain very special. There are still hundreds of spots away from the crowds, and Greek islanders remain among the most charming people in the world. Even on the most-developed island, a short journey inland, away from the smell of sun-tan oil and the beat of the disco, takes you back to villages and landscapes largely unaffected by the holiday boom.

Islanders overseas

Millions of Greeks left their homeland during the 19th century, and many islands which once numbered their inhabitants in tens of thousands have quite literally been decimated. Migrants from any island tended to head for the same destination, and almost all dreamed of returning when their fortune was made. Not all succeeded, but on Sámos and Kýthira you will hear lots of Greek-Australian accents, Kálymnos and Chálki have links with Florida, Ikaría and Lésvos with the US and Canada, and on Kárpathos you may even meet Greek returnees from Kenya and Sudan.

Island personality

People who have met Greeks overseas hustling to make their fortune are sometimes surprised to see how laid-back they seem to be in their natural habitat. That's partly because much of the hard work of an island day is done in the early morning hours, when most visitors are still asleep. Partly, too, islanders are blessed with a sunny mentality that takes life as it comes – though they can drive a hard bargain when they want to.

Ancient ancestors?

You may well meet Greeks bearing ancient names – Aristotle and Socrates are popular – but unsurprisingly modern Greeks have not much in common with their ancestors of more than 2,000 years ago. There is a real pride in their achievements, but if Greeks do look back on a Hellenic Golden Age, it is the 1,000-year Byzantine Empire of Constantine the Great and his heirs.

On smaller, less prosperous islands like Síkinos, farming is primitive

Politics

Since 1974 Greece has been a parliamentary democracy with an elected president whose role is mainly ceremonial. Real power is in the hands of an elected prime minister.

Islanders share the nationwide passion for politics, and general elections take on a festive air of family reunion. The Civil War of 1946–9, fought on the mainland, had less impact on islanders, but memories of oppression then, and during the 1967–74 military junta, are still quite fresh.

Oil and troubled waters

Also fresh in the memory is the Turkish invasion of Cyprus in 1974. Since small oil reserves were discovered in the northeast Aegean, Turkey has claimed mineral rights below the continental shelf. This, like anything which touches on Greek sovereignty, is a live political issue, and the substantial Greek military presence on islands near the Turkish coast is a constant reminder of the friction between the countries.

Political parties

Political power is highly centralised, and islanders almost always feel that they are not getting a fair shake from Athens when it comes to investment in infrastructure. This resentment is sometimes fostered by rash campaign promises along the lines of 'vote for us and we'll build you an airport!'

Greece has two major political parties, the right-wing Nea Dimokratia (New Democracy) and the left-wing PASOK (Pan-Hellenic Socialist Alliance). Three smaller parties, the centrist Politiki Anoikti ('Political Spring'), the old style KKE (Greek Communist Party) and a reformed KKE offshoot, the Central Democratic Renewal Party are also represented.

There's as much variety in island politics as in every other aspect of life in the archipelago. Ikaría and Lésvos, remain strongly left-wing despite the decline of the Communist Party elsewhere in Greece, while others, like Chíos, lean to the right.

A KKE poster urges Greece to pull out of the European Union

FIRST STEPS

'Many be the summer mornings
When with what pleasure, with what delight
You enter harbours never seen before.'
C P CAVAFY
(1863–1933), *Ithaka*

First Steps

Ancient Greece

You will find relics of the ancient world scattered throughout the islands, but Crete and the Aegean island groups offer the richest treasure trove. Sites guaranteed not to disappoint include Knosós, Faistós and Górtys on Crete (see pages 80–1); Líndos, Ialýssos and the Temple of Apollo on Rhodes (see pages 102–7) ; the Agorá and Asklipion on Kós (see pages 110–11); the Sanctuary of the Great Gods on Samothráki (see pages 124–5); Akrotíri on Thíra (Santoríni)(see pages 66–7) and perhaps most of all the complex of shrines and sanctuaries on Dílos (see pages 60–1 and 74–5).

Some carefully signposted sites have little more than a few scattered column-drums or foundations to mark them, and all have suffered the ravages of up to 4,000 years of natural disasters, war, invasion and neglect. A specialist guidebook or knowledgeable guide is vital if you want to make the most of your sightseeing, helping the mind's eye to see the palaces and temples as they once were.

Beaches

The Greek islands offer every kind of beach, from tiny, hard-to-reach coves of white pebbles to sweeps of sand lined with loungers and parasols. There are long sandy beaches on Corfu and its Ionian neighbours, Zákynthos and Kefalloniá, on Páros and Mýkonos, on the north coast of Crete and on Rhodes, Sámos and Kós. Thíra (Santoríni)has beaches of black volcanic sand (which can get painfully hot under midsummer sun). Best of all, perhaps, is popular Skíathos, which has dozens of soft sandy beaches.

Castles

Venetians, Turks, Genoese and Crusaders left cragtop castles towering over key harbours everywhere. Some, like those on Corfu and Léros, are still used by the Greek military. Among the most impressive are Kýthira's Venetian keep, the castles of the Gattelusi on Lésvos, the fortresses of the Knights of St John on Kós, and the fortified Monastery of St John the Divine on Pátmos.

Historic towns

The Old Town of Rhodes with its massive fortifications, labyrinth of alleys, and restored palace is the most striking of island capitals. Chaniá and Réthymno on Crete, and the island capital on Kós, are all interesting blends of ancient and medieval history with an exotic

Greek island beaches may be vast sweeps of sand or tiny pebbly coves

Mighty medieval fortresses, like this one at Mólivos on Lésvos, tower over many island towns

whiff of the east. Náxos Town, the capital of Náxos, with its whitewashed, hidden citadel of the Sanudo dukes, is another delight. Corfu Town offers a different history, with reminders of Venice, revolutionary France and Victorian England.

Picturesque villages

The boxy white houses and blue-domed churches of so many postcards are found in the Cyclades group. The island capital almost always bears the name of the island itself though islanders usually just call it Chóra (the market-village). The prettiest include the dramatic crater-edge Chóra on Thíra (Santoríni), the harbourside Chóras of Mýkonos and Páros, and the hilltop Chóra of Folégandros. Astypálaia and Amorgós have lovely white villages, too.

For a taste of a different village style, visit Mólivos on Lésvos with its tall, Turkish-style homes; the Argo-Saronic islands and their sea-captains' mansions; or Líndos on Rhodes with its pebble-mosaic courtyards.

When to go

The islands are most crowded in July and August. To avoid the crowds and the most intense heat visit from mid-April to mid-June or in September and early October. Spring has the added beauty of red, yellow and purple wild flowers, and in September the sea is still deliciously warm. The weather stays balmy into November, but becomes wet and windy. Most tourism facilities close by the end of October, and the smaller islands have very little to offer visitors from November to March.

Fast, modern ferries connect the islands with each other and with ports all over the mainland

ISLAND TO ISLAND

The arrival of the ferry is the high point of the day in a harbour village, and as an ant-like parade of backpackers and locals pours off the boat, accompanied with much shouting, gesticulating and sounding of horns by a cavalcade of trucks, cars and motorcycles, chaos seems to reign. In fact, it's all very organised, and allowing for wind and weather it's surprising how punctual most ferries are. Timetables are issued close to the beginning of the tourist season and can be difficult to get hold of outside Greece. Thomas Cook publishes a guide to Greek ferry services, *Greek Island Hopping* by Frewin Poffley, which gives schedules for every ferry service, descriptions of the ships, detailed maps and sightseeing information about the islands themselves.

Buying a ticket

Harbourside agencies sell tickets, but each agency represents a different line. Where several lines operate, fares will be much the same but schedules differ, and the agency is unlikely to tell you about the services of a competing ferry. Ask around to be sure, or inquire at the Port Police office (Limenarchion), where an up-to-date timetable will be displayed. Port police officers wear natty white uniforms. If you plan to island hop, always allow for delays: strong winds can stop sailings for 24 hours or more and ferry schedules change from month to month.

Ferry, hydrofoil or catamaran?

Main-line ferries are big, fast and modern, with Pullman-seated lounges available for passengers buying the cheapest fare (still often, and misleadingly, called 'deck class'). Shorter hops may be served by smaller ferries with fewer facilities, but drinks and snacks are always available on board. Hydrofoils offer a speedy, costlier alternative on many routes in summer, especially in the Dodecanese, Argo-Saronic and Cyclades groups. Fast catamarans also run from Rhodes to several Dodecanese islands. Beware however that both of these may provide quite a rough ride as they bounce across the wavetops at high speed.

Flying
Olympic Aviation, the internal wing of Olympic Airways, operates flights from Athens to many islands and some inter-island flights. Fares are relatively cheap and waiting lists are long. It's best to book before leaving home and vital to reconfirm your reservation. Beware that Athens airport is particularly chaotic so check in as early as possible and be prepared for problems.

GETTING AROUND
Buses
The island bus, usually irregular, elderly, but packed with islanders and visitors, is an institution. Buses go anywhere there is a road, but out-of-the-way villages may have only one bus a day, so beware of being stranded.

Boats
On the most popular holiday islands small motorboats ply between the main villages and resorts and the best beaches. Self-drive motorboats can be hired on some islands, including Corfu and Skíathos.

Cars
Cars, beach-buggies or jeeps can be hired almost everywhere. Car hire in Greece is relatively expensive, and soft-top cars cost more. Roads are often poorly-surfaced and care is needed on the many sharp bends and steep hills. Make sure your insurance covers you fully for damage to the vehicle (though damage to the underside and to tyres will always be your responsibility).

Cycling
Bikes are for hire on some islands and are ideal for short trips. Longer journeys can be hilly and hot.

Hitch-hiking
Islanders are quite generous with rides, but you may have to wait for hours where vehicles are few.

Mopeds and motorcycles
Thousands of holidaymakers are injured and some are killed each year riding rented motorcycles. They are often under-maintained and few operators offer helmets or basic instruction. Island roads and island traffic are dangerous to the inexperienced rider. If you have not ridden before, do not do so.

Taxis
Taxis are quite cheap and are a very useful way of getting around. They await each ferry and are quickly snapped up. Be first ashore (you'll have to be pushy!) to be sure of getting one.

Riding without helmets or protective clothing is hazardous; always take great care

LANGUAGE, MANNERS AND CUSTOMS
Hospitality

Island hospitality is legendary. Away from the boom-town resorts you may be surprised by a carafe of retsina sent to your table by a complete stranger or a gift of fruit from an island orchard and even in the most popular resorts philoxenia ('love of guests') is only dying out very slowly as the tourism profit motive asserts itself.

Queuing

Queuing for transport is unheard of. Boarding a bus or a ferry is a race for seats and disembarking too is a race for waiting taxis. In banks or post offices, queues do form, though some Greeks will still push in ahead of tourists.

Dress code

Topless sunbathing is now accepted on even the most public beaches. Nudity however is officially illegal. It is sanctioned on designated beaches, but it will offend on a town or resort beach. Shorts and T-shirts are acceptable summer wear everywhere, but knees and arms must be covered when visiting monasteries.

Women travellers

Greek men nearly always feel that a woman is flattered by their attention, but an unambiguous 'no' is usually a sufficient deterrent to would-be romeos. You are more likely to be harassed by mainland Greek or foreign visitors than by islanders.

Language

The Greek language and alphabet can be intimidating, but a little Greek goes a very long way. Greeks believe that their language is almost impossible for foreigners to learn and knowledge of a few simple phrases will be extravagantly praised. English and German are widely spoken by islanders as a result of tourism, emigration and service in the merchant navy.

Islanders use plenty of body language which can be helpful or confusing. A backward jerk of the head, which looks like a nod, is actually a 'no', accompanied for emphasis by a click of the tongue. A rapid side-to-side shake of the head means anything from 'I don't understand' to 'What can I do for you?'

Rules against topless nudism and 'improper dress' are more often ignored than obeyed

'Where mythology walks in a wave
And the islands are.'
LAWRENCE DURRELL
(1912–90), Matapan

Iónia Nisiá
(Ionian Islands)

*T*he Ionian islands stretch down Greece's west coast, from Corfu in the north to Kýthira, sitting alone off the southern tip of mainland Greece. The group includes several of Greece's most popular holiday isles, and it's easy to see why. Some of the country's best sandy beaches are to be found here and landscapes are greener and easier on the eye than those of many Aegean islands.

Reliable summer winds make the Ionians a favourite for yachties and windsurfers, while the green and hilly hinterlands appeal to walkers and explorers.

Dramatic medieval harbour and hilltop fortresses make up for a dearth of more ancient sites, and the attractions of mainland Greece, within sight of each island, are easy to reach.

Ionian harbours and market towns bustle with colourful everyday life, and Corfu Town, the administrative capital of the group, is one of the most charming of island capitals. Unfortunately earthquakes – the most recent in 1953 – have deprived the other islands of the type of picturesque village homes which delight visitors to other Greek isles.

There are seven main islands in the group, plus a scattering of tiny satellite islets, and Greeks often refer to them collectively as the Heptanissia (the Seven Islands). Six are cheek by jowl in the northwest: Kýthira, the joker in the pack, is far away to the south. Although close to each other, these are not the easiest of islands for hopping, which often involves a zig-zag route; crossing to the nearest mainland port, taking a bus to another mainland harbour, then taking another ferry.

White walls at Avlemonas stand out against a barren hillside

IONIAN ISLANDS

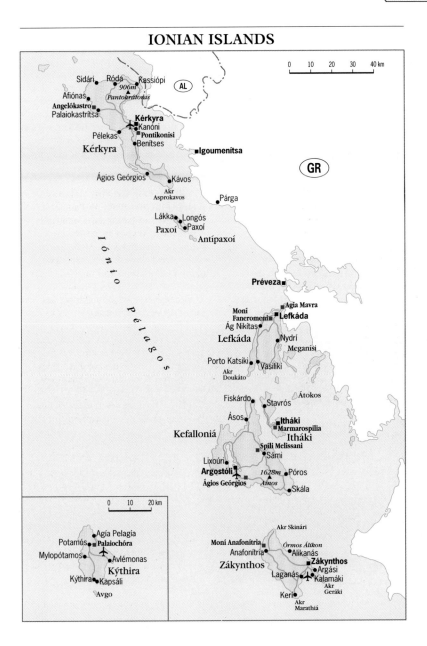

0   10   20   30   40 km

Sidári   Róda   Kassiópi   AL
906m   *Pantokrátoras*
Afiónas
Angelókastro
Palaiokastrítsa
   Kérkyra
   Kanóni
Pélekas   **Pontikonísi**
   Benítses
Kérkyra
   ■Igoumenítsa

   GR

Ágios Geórgios   Kávos
   Akr
   Asprokavos   Párga

Lákka   Longós
   Paxoí
Paxoí
   Antípaxoí

Iónio

Pélagos

   Préveza■

   Agia Mavra
Moní   ■**Lefkáda**
Faneromeni
Ág Nikítas
   Lefkáda   Nydrí
   Meganísi
Porto Katsiki   Vasilikí
   Akr
   Doukáto

Fiskárdo   Átokos
   Stavrós
Ásos   ■**Itháki**
Kefalloniá   ■Marmarospilia
   Itháki
   Spíli Melissani
Lixoúri   Sámi
Argostóli   1628m   Póros
Ágios Geórgios   *Aínos*
   Skála

0   10   20 km

   Agía Pelagía
Potamós   ■**Palaiochóra**
Mylopótamos   Avlémonas
   Kýthira
Kýthira   Kapsáli
   Avgo

   Akr Skinári
Moní Anafonítria   *Órmos Álikon*
Anafonítria   Alikanás
Zákynthos   ■**Zákynthos**
   Argási
Laganás   Kalamáki
   Akr
Kerí   Geráki
   Akr
   Marathiá

ANTÍPAXOÍ (ANTIPAXOS)

See page 38.

KÉRKYRA (CORFU)

Corfu is an island of rolling green farmland, vineyards and orange groves, all under the looming bulk of Mount Pantokrátoras. The second largest of the Ionian islands, it is by far the most popular – in fact, it is one of the most popular holiday islands in Greece, with resorts on every beach along its 217km coastline. Most of these are catering for the cheap and cheerful end of the package tour market.

The island capital, midway along the east coast, is delightful – and surprisingly untouristy, as it has no beaches of its own and most visitors stay at one of the resorts and visit the town only on a day trip.

Inland and in the island's farmlands and northern hills, quiet landscapes and rural villages are quite untouched too.

Corfu's most spectacular beaches and prettiest coastal scenery are on the island's long west coast. The heaviest development has been on the east coast, either side of Corfu Town and its airport, and you will find more space and solitude on the west, as well as glowing sunsets over the Iónio Pélagos (Ionian Sea).

Corfu is long and thin, and the grey slopes of the 906m Mount Pantokrátoras dominate its wider northern end, with woods giving way to open hillsides. From these, and even from the east coast beaches, you have a clear view of the Píndos mountains on the

Kassiópi's harbourside and streets are lined with shops, cafés and restaurants

Greek mainland, only a couple of hours away by boat, and of the even closer Albanian coast, which is less than a kilometre away from Corfu at its closest point.

Part of the Byzantine Empire from the 4th century AD, Corfu was seized by Venice in 1205 and stayed in Venetian hands, resisting several Turkish assaults, until 1797, when Napoleon conquered it for France. In 1814 France was ousted by Britain and the following year the island and its Ionian neighbours became a British protectorate. The Union Jack was hauled down in 1864 and the islands joined the Kingdom of Greece.

The Venetians left an Italianate island capital and a handful of Renaissance churches. The French bestowed a stylish arcade of shops and cafés in Corfu Town and the British legacy includes a collection of grand public buildings and a taste for cricket and ginger beer.

ÁGIOS GEÓRGIOS (NORTH)

Just to be confusing, Corfu has two beaches officially called Ágios Geórgios, both on the west coast. However this one, to the north, is better known as Ágios Giórgiou which at least provides a slight differentiation. It is a great sweep of sand within a vast bay and is relatively undeveloped.
25km northwest of Corfu Town.

ÁGIOS GEÓRGIOS (SOUTH)

This Ágios Geórgios, far to the south, is a giant expanse of majestic sand-dunes

Colourful pedaloes and beach umbrellas brighten popular Ágios Geórgios beach

with a number of new holiday hotels scattered along it. These are unenchanting, but the beach is so huge that it always offers potential for solitude.
35km southwest of Corfu Town.

KASSIÓPI

A natural, lagoon-like harbour is the chief attraction of this fishing village-turned-resort on the north coast. Across the eastern strait are fine views to the rugged badlands of the Albanian mountains.

The harbour is lined with cafés and restaurants. There are coves and beaches to either side, accessible by regular boat services.
30km north of Corfu Town.

Kástro (Castle)

The shattered walls of an early medieval Venetian castle sit on the hillside just north of Kassiópi village centre overlooking Kassiópi harbour.
Freely accessible.

Cafés along the Spianada in Corfu Town have a Parisian flair

KÁVOS

Set among gentle farmland, Kávos has mushroomed from a quiet fishing hamlet to a fully-fledged resort with scores of bars and discos competing to offer the liveliest happy-hour and the strongest cocktails. The huge 2 to 3km sweep of east-facing beach with its gently-shelving sands is the main daytime attraction.
45km south of Corfu Town.

KÉRKYRA (Corfu Town)

The charming island capital has a population of around 40,000 and with its faded rose and ochre stucco buildings complete with wooden shutters, wrought-iron balconies, and flights of stone steps it looks very Italian. British and French occupiers have also left their mark. The picturesque Campiello quarter was built on a headland guarded by two fortresses, under the Venetians. It rises south of the ferry harbour, with the open space of the Spianada park on its east side, the Palaio Frourio (Old Fortress) on an eastern crag, and the Neo Frourio (New Fortress) to the north, near the harbour.
East coast of Corfu.

Arkheologiko Moussío (Archaeological Museum)

Finds from local sites. Highlights include the Gorgon from the Temple of Artemis and a 7th-century BC stone lion.
Vraila 5 (tel: 0661 30680). Open: Tuesday to Sunday 8.30am–3pm. Admission charge.

Ágios Spiridon

Built in 1596, the church houses the silver-encased body of the island's patron saint, credited not only with saving Corfu from the plague in 1630 and invading Turks in 1716, but also from Italian bombs in World War II. It also features an elaborate painted ceiling.
Platía Ágios Spiridou. Open: daily. Admission free.

Mitropoleos
The cathedral in the old quarter, built in 1577, houses the coffin of the Byzantine Empress Theodora, who was canonised in the 9th century.
Platía Mitropoleou. Open: daily. Admission free.

Moussío Solomos (Solomos Museum)
The former home of the Greek poet laureate, Dionysos Solomos (1786–1857), with a small collection of memorabilia.
Arseniou 41. Open: Monday to Friday 5pm–8pm. Admission charge.

Neo Frourio (New Fortress)
This angular stone fortress built between the 16th and 19th centuries is still used as a Greek naval headquarters.
Overlooking the ferry harbour. Closed to visitors.

Palaio Frourio (Old Fortress)
This 16th-century castle on twin crags is severed from the city by a sea-moat. There are fine views from its highest turret, and on summer evenings it is used for dramatic sound and light performances (see page 165).
Cross bridge east of Spianada. Open: 15 May–30 September, 9am–8pm. No admission charge. Sound and light show, four times a week, 8pm. Admission charge.

Palace of St Michael and St George (Museum of Asiatic Art)
The elegant 19th-century palace, built for the British Governors and later used by the Greek monarchy, was refurbished for the 1994 European Summit and houses a collection of Oriental artefacts.
North end of the Spianada (tel: 0661 23124). Open: Tuesday to Sunday 8.30am–3pm. Admission charge.

A vividly coloured icon of the sainted Byzantine Empress Theodora adorns Corfu's cathedral

Rotonda
A 19th-century memorial in the classical Ionian mode to Sir Thomas Maitland, first British governor of the Ionian protectorate between 1815 and 1824.
South end of the Spianada.

Spianada
The most elegant public square in the Greek islands, Spianada is lined on one side by an arcade of stylish cafés, built by the French between 1807 and 1814. Look for the statue of Ioannis Capodistrias (1776–1831), Greece's first president. Cricket is still played on the huge green.
Centre of Corfu Town, 750m from harbour.

Vlachérne
Postcards of this delightful if very commercialised monastery islet linked to the Kanóni beach by a 25m causeway manage to exclude the airport runway immediately inland.
Kanóni, 4km from town centre. Open: daily. Admission free, donations welcomed.

The turquoise waters of Palaiokastrítsa are one of the most beautiful sights on Corfu

PALAIOKASTRÍTSA

Steep, pine-wooded slopes and limestone crags surround this gorgeous double bay, the prettiest scene on Corfu with two small, crowded beaches separated by a towering headland. There are lots of smaller coves and beaches to either side, and motorboats ply frequently to these from the Palaiokastrítsa pier.

Palaiokastrítsa has been renowned as a beauty spot since the British occupation, when army engineers built the first road there from Corfu Town. Famous visitors included the painter and nonsense poet Edward Lear (1812–88), who made a number of sketches and watercolours of Palaiokastrítsa and other island scenes.

26km northwest of Corfu Town.

Angelókastro

On a giddy peak above the sea sits the shell of a square-sided Byzantine keep which hides a tiny whitewashed chapel. It is named not for the angels but for Michael I Angelos, the 13th-century Byzantine Despot of Ípeiros (Epirus) and Corfu, who built it.

11km north of Palaiokastrítsa. Freely accessible.

Zoodochos Pigi Monastery

This 18th-century fortress-like whitewashed monastery contains a miracle-working 12th-century icon of the Virgin. The rock you can see on the horizon is said to be a pirate ship turned to stone by the Virgin to protect her monastery from raiders.

On the Ágios Nikólaos promontory. Open: daily. Admission charge (candle purchase obligatory).

PANTOKRÁTOR ÓROS
(Mount Pantokrátoras)

The 906m-high Pantokrátoras massif dominates northeast Corfu, tempting walkers and explorers. You can drive almost all the way to the top, leaving your car at the hill village of Petáleia and walking the last 2km on a rough footpath. Alternatively, walking to the summit from the prettily dilapidated hamlet of Perítheia takes one to one and a half hours. It's well worth it for the superb panoramic view of the whole island spread out below. The treeless slopes of Albania lie to the east and the Píndos ranges extend into Epirus on the Greek mainland further south.

25 to 30km north of Corfu Town.

PONTIKONISI

Just offshore, this islet with its miniature monastery is in all the postcards and is said to be the petrified remains of the ship of the Homeric hero Odysseus, turned to stone by the angry sea-god Poseidon.

750m from Kanóni, 4km from Corfu Town centre. Excursion boats daily from most resorts.

RÓDA

Midway along the north coast of the island, Róda has one of the best beaches in the area. As a result it has grown into a rather sprawling resort, but there is still room to escape from the crowds and it makes a pleasant base for exploring Pantokrátoras and the northern hinterland.

37km northwest of Corfu Town.

SIDÁRI

Like Róda, Sidári has grown into an extensive resort thanks to a long sandy beach and warm shallow water.

48km northwest of Corfu Town.

Canal d'Amour (Channel of Love)

According to local legend the channel, a long, rocky inlet whose cliffs are eroded into weird shapes, guarantees a husband to any young woman who takes a dip in it.

2km west of Sidári.

ITHÁKI (ITHACA)

Tiny Itháki (just under 100sq km) is best known as the legendary home of Odysseus (Ulysses) and his goal in his long journey home from the siege of Troy. Another famous visitor, Lord Byron (1788–1824), was so charmed by the island that he toyed with the idea of buying it.

Itháki is a narrow island, about 20km long from north to south and cut almost in two by the Kólpos Mólou (Gulf of Molos). This opening on the east coast has sheltered waters and steady breezes which make the island a delight for dinghy-sailors and windsurfers. The island's sand-and-pebble beaches are small but uncrowded and usually clean.
2km east of Kefalloniá.

ITHÁKI TOWN (VATHI)

Itháki's capital, home to more than 2,000 of its 3,600 people, was rebuilt after the 1953 earthquake. Its charm owes more to its superbly scenic site, on a near-landlocked inlet surrounded by steep hills, than to any architectural merit.
At the inner end of a southern arm of the Gulf of Molos.

Marmarospilia (Cave of the Nymphs)
Odysseus is said to have hidden his treasure in this limestone sea-cavern.
3km southwest of Itháki Town. Freely accessible.

Sarakiniko and Skinos
The best beaches on Itháki are between these headlands on the east coast, reached on foot or by small boats from Itháki Town.
2 to 5km northeast of Itháki Town.

KEFALLONIÁ

Biggest of the Ionian group, Kefalloniá is an island of varied landscapes, a near-tropical study in vivid turquoise, green and brilliant white.

On the northwest coast, steep cliffs plummet towards white pebble beaches and the most brilliantly coloured blue sea in Greece, while the lower Kefallonián slopes are covered with citrus trees, olive groves and vineyards. Robola wine, made from these grapes, is reckoned to be

Fiskárdo is arguably the prettiest village on Kefalloniá, and a popular yacht harbour among the best in Greece.

The best beaches – long, sandy and uncrowded – are on the south coast, where there are several small resorts. Like its neighbours, Kefalloniá suffered in the 1953 earthquake and most of its communities were rebuilt after then.

The blue lagoon of Kefalloniá is fed by endless underground springs

ÁGIOS GEÓRGIOS

The hulking hilltop fortress of Ágios Geórgios stands guard over southern Kefalloniá. Built in 1300 by the Orsini family, the island's Venetian rulers, it was their capital until 1757, when they felt secure enough from Turkish invasion to move down to Argostóli. Its walls once sheltered 15,000 people and the shells of houses and churches still stand within the imposing ramparts.

12km southeast of Argostóli.

ARGOSTÓLI

The island's capital is on a natural west-coast harbour sheltered by the Paliki peninsula. Entry is by an impressive 650m causeway built in the early 19th-century, when the island was ruled by Britain.

Moussío Arkheologiko (Archaeological Museum)

Pottery and other finds from around the island.

Veryoti 89. Open: Tuesday to Sunday 8.30am–3pm. Admission charge.

Moussío Koryialeniou (Korgialenios Museum)

A vivid collection including mock-ups of Venetian nobles' homes and artisans'

workshops, as well as costumes and illustrations of a bygone way of life in Argostóli.

Veryoti 41. Open: Monday to Saturday 9am–1pm and 6pm–8pm (summer); Monday to Saturday 8am–2.30pm (winter). Admission charge.

FISKÁRDO

Named after the Sicilian Norman baron Robert Guiscard who died here in 1085, this is the prettiest village on Kefalloniá and is the only significant survivor of the 1953 earthquake. Gracious old houses and a yacht-filled harbour add to its charm.

On the northern tip of the island, 53km from Argostóli.

SPÍLI MELISSANI (MELISSANI CAVE)

An underground blue lagoon is fed by natural tunnels which, amazingly, stretch far beneath the island to emerge near Argostóli.

Access by boat. 3km northwest of Sámi, on the east coast. Open: daily 8am–sunset. Admission charge.

KÝTHIRA

Rocky and remote, Kýthira guards the channel linking the Aegean with the open Mediterranean, not far from the southernmost point of the mainland (it is administered with the Argo-Saronic group of islands). Its high, flat-topped outline is instantly recognisable to anyone who has seen the film *The Guns of Navarone*, for which it was a location.

Kýthira's westward aspects, with their clifftop views out to an empty horizon, appear almost Atlantic. It's an empty island, all but 3,400 of its inhabitants having left for Australia around the turn of the century, and it feels bigger than its 278sq km. High sea-cliffs thrust up to a windswept plateau of thorn-trees, studded with dabs of cultivated greenery, and most of the upland villages are hidden in little sheltered valleys.

This is an island for anyone looking for peace and quiet – except in July and August, when it bustles with Greek-Australian emigrants visiting stay-at-home relatives.
20km south of Akr Maléas (Cape Malea); 60km north of Crete.

AGÍA PELAGÍA

The northernmost of Kýthira's two harbour-villages, this is the less interesting of the pair, with a narrow, gritty beach at the foot of its rocky hillsides. However it does have more frequent ferry and hydrofoil connections to the mainland than the southern port.
18km north of Kýthira Town.

KAPSÁLI

The port of Kapsáli enjoys clean, coarse-sand beaches on two pocket-sized bays, a string of tavernas and a row of pretty white houses with flower-filled gardens.

It is overlooked by the magical silhouette (especially lovely at dusk) of Kýthira Town. Out to sea is Avgo, the egg-shaped sea-rock said to be the egg from which Aphrodite, goddess of love and beauty, hatched.
2km south of Kýthira Town.

KÝTHIRA TOWN

This lovely clifftop village with its whitewashed houses and narrow twisty streets, belongs much more to the Cyclades than to the Ionian. The best place to admire its position if from below at Kapsáli.
On the southern tip of the island.

Kástro (Castle)

The prettiest castle in the islands perches on the village's highest point. Inside there are the picturesque shells of the inner keep, a couple of small churches and half a dozen rusting iron cannons of Napoleonic provenance (three of them carrying British insignia). The view is uplifting, with Avgo close inshore and the outline of Kýthira's tiny and almost uninhabited satellite, Antikýthira, on the southern horizon. Just below the castle, a plaque marks the birthplace of the poet and Orientalist Lafkadio Hearne (1850–1904).
100m from the village centre, at the end of the main street. Freely accessible.

MYLOPÓTAMOS

Hidden in a ravine below the level of the dry plateau, Mylopótamos is pleasantly green and secret, with a burbling stream tumbling into a cool oasis-like grotto.
6km north of Kýthira Town.

Káto Chóra

The crest of Venice, the Lion of St Mark, is carved above the great gateway of this charming and neglected miniature fortress. Arched buildings within the square of battlements are gradually falling into ruin.

7km west of Mylopótamos. Freely accessible.

Spíli Agía Sofia (Cave of the Holy Wisdom)

The entrance to this chilly hillside grotto was once a church and still carries Byzantine frescos. Further in, the 250m cave system is adorned with spikes and pinnacles of limestone.

3km from Mylopótamos. Open: summer only 3pm–5pm. Admission charge.

PALAIOCHÓRA

The Byzantine island capital is spectacularly sited with 100m cliffs on three sides, hidden from the sea to protect it from raiders. This did not save it from sacking by the feared Turkish pirate Barbarossa in 1537 and it was never rebuilt. Its ruins include a small castle and the shells of dozens of churches.

3km east of Potamós, 15km north of Kýthira Town.

Kýthira castle. Views from here (inset) include Kapsáli's two bays

LEFKÁDA (LEVKAS)

Levkas means white, and the bare mountain slopes of the hinterland are indeed whitish, with only a few pine trees clinging to their higher flanks. Around and below the central mountains, Levkas is a verdant, pretty island, with fertile farmlands and hundreds of blue beehives scattered among the goat pasture.

Only 650m separate Levkas from the mainland and the narrow strait is crossed by a swing-bridge and a causeway guarded by fortifications.

The east coast of the island faces on to a broad, calm expanse of water sheltered by the mainland and the offshore island of Meganísi. One of the tiny wooded islets here was the former hideaway of the millionaire Onassis family. This is a favourite area for yachts and windsurfers.

The west coast is more rugged, with cliffs and steep slopes rising above a string of white sandy beaches formed by the pounding of winter storms.

In the turbulent Middle Ages Levkas changed hands even more frequently than most Greek islands. It was fought over by the Normans of Sicily and the Byzantine Empire in the 11th century, taken by the Venetians in 1331, and ruled by Angevin Franks from 1362 until 1467, when it became the only Ionian island to be occupied by the Ottoman Turks. In 1684 it was reconquered by Venice and from then on shared the fortunes of its Ionian neighbours, with a brief interval of Russian control between 1807 and 1814. *35km from Áktio airport, 40km southwest of the mainland port of Préveza.*

ÁGIOS NIKÍTAS

There are excellent beaches either side of this tiny fishing village and resort. Small boats commute between Ágios Nikítas and its satellite beaches several times a day in summer.
On the west coast, 8km southwest of Levkas Town.

AKR DOUKÁTO (PETRA LEVKAS)

The legendary poetess Sappho (*c*600BC) is said to have thrown herself from this dramatic 70m-high white cliff, as the victim of unrequited love. Traces of a 7th-century BC Temple of Apollo can be seen next to the lighthouse on the island's southernmost tip.
46km south of Levkas Town.

LEFKÁDA (LEVKAS TOWN)

Levelled by the 1953 quake, Levkas Town has been patchily rebuilt and has an eccentric

Thick woodlands stretch down to the sea on Levkas's south coast

Porto Katsiki's crescent of white sand can be reached by rugged road or by boat

charm. The upper stories of many houses are built of bright-painted corrugated iron (an anti-earthquake ploy). The town faces inland, away from its lagoon, and hardly feels like a harbour town. Instead, it's more like an inland farming village. Repeated earthquakes have left it with little historic interest, but a medieval castle and monastery lie near by.
Northwest coast.

Agía Mavra

The 14th-century fortress of the Orsinis, built to guard the approaches to the island, is complemented by ramparts built in 1807 by the Russians, who briefly occupied Levkas between the ousting of France and the British takeover.
1km from Levkas Town, on the islet midway along the causeway.

Moní Faneromeni (Faneromeni Monastery)

This deserted monastery dates from the 16th century and still possesses its wooden simantron, the heavy wooden bar beaten with a hammer to call the monks to prayer.
3km southwest of Levkas Town on the road to Ágios Nikítas.

NYDRÍ (NIDRI)

Midway down the east coast, Nydrí stands on a mirror-like lagoon which is punctuated by tree-tufted islands and, in summer, covered with the white and day-glo sails of yachts and windsurfers. There are some pleasant walks in the hilly farming country inland, and a long narrow beach stretches in front of the village.
17km southwest of Levkas Town.

PORTO KATSIKI

One of the most spectacular beaches in all the islands, this white crescent of coarse sand lies beneath a half-circle of jagged cliffs. It can be reached by a nerve-wracking rough jeep road or more comfortably by boat from Ágios Nikítas.
40km southwest of Levkas Town.

PAXOÍ (PAXOS)

Measuring only 25sq km, Paxos is the smallest of the Ionian islands. It is also the closest to Corfu and is therefore a favourite day-trip destination. Regular ferries also run to Párga, the attractive mainland port resort, less than two hours away by boat.

Paxos's low hills are entirely cloaked in the silver-grey of some 300,000 olive trees. Here and there among the groves you can spot a ruined farmhouse or olive-mill. There is plenty of shade beneath the olives, and as the island is only 270m at its highest point and 10km from end to end it is a favourite for walkers. Beaches are pebbly and tiny, and dotted at frequent intervals round the island's 25km shoreline. The island's three tiny villages are also on the coast.

Paxos has few claims to historical fame, but Mark Anthony and Cleopatra are said to have spent their last night together on the island before sailing to defeat at the hands of Octavian at the sea-battle of Actium (31BC), 100km south of Paxos.
20km south of Corfu; 25km west of Párga on the mainland.

ANTÍPAXOÍ (ANTIPAXOS)

Paxos's tiny satellite achieves the startling feat of making its bigger neighbour look both busy and cosmopolitan. A hundred or so inhabitants cultivate small terraced vineyards and a handful of tavernas make a good living in summer from day-trippers who come by boat from Paxos and Corfu. The beach at Vrikes, the island's tiny village, is crowded when the boats come in, but for a bit more solitude you can easily walk to a clutch of quiet pebble-and-sand coves on Antipaxos's south coast.
5km south of Paxos.

LÁKKA

Two curving promontories almost enclose Lákka's natural harbour. Gentle morning breezes and strong, constant afternoon winds make it one of Greece's premier windsurfing training centres. There is a pebbly beach on the west side of the bay.
12km northwest of Paxos Town.

LONGÓS

Longós sits on an east-facing mirror-like lagoon. A handful of villas and cafés crowd around the village square and narrow quayside, from which café tables

Longós (left) and Paxos Town (right) are the best places to stay on Paxos

have to be moved when the daily bus wants to squeeze by. There are clean, pebbly coves south of the village.
10km north of Paxos Town.

PAXOÍ (PAXOS TOWN/GAIOS)

Half of Paxos's islanders, about 1,200 people, live in the island's main village, a perfect Italianate island capital on a miniature scale, built around a flagstoned dockside square with a church and campanile. It is hidden away from the open sea by two islets, Panagía and Ágios Nikólaos, so that its harbour channel is more like a sheltered lake.
On the northeast coast at the southern end of Paxos.

OLIVES AND ISLANDERS

The silvery leaves of olive trees seem to cover almost every square metre of Paxos. Olives are part of Greece's heritage, grown from the earliest times as part of the 'Mediterranean triad' which also included grapes and grain. Olive trees are very long-lived and are valuable heirlooms. Like earmarks on sheep, numbers and initials painted on the trunk tell who each tree belongs to. A family may have dozens of trees scattered in ones and twos all over an island.
Trees are often owned independently of the land they grow on, and the landowner must allow access for harvesting and pruning. The olive tree yields more fruit if pruned annually, and the slow-burning trimmings make excellent winter firewood. In the old days islanders made bowls, plates and spoons from close-grained olive wood, and it is still used in boat-building.

ZÁKYNTHOS (ZANTE)

After Corfu, Zákynthos is the most popular of the Ionian holiday islands, and no wonder. Inland, the island is a pastoral chequerboard of green vineyards, fruit orchards and groves of almonds, grain fields and pastureland. In spring, when its hills and roadsides are ablaze with wild blooms, it's easy to see why the Venetians called it *Fior di Levante* – the Flower of the Levant.

ARGÁSI

The popularity of this crowded resort is hard to explain, as its beach, a narrow strip of sand mixed with shingle does not come up to the standard of other sunbathing stretches on Zákynthos. However, with lots of bars and tavernas and several discos, Argási's nightlife runs noisy Laganás a close second.

LAGANÁS

Zákynthos's southeast coast is a broad bight, with Kólpos Lagana (the Laganás Gulf), bounded by two rocky headlands, Akr Marathiá in the southwest and Akr Geráki in the east. Midway between the two is the tourism boom town of Laganás, which in a few years has grown from a tiny collection of fishermen's cottages to a thriving resort full of hotels, tavernas and bars. East of Laganás, a superb sandy beach stretches for almost 4km to Kalamáki, a smaller resort spread out among fields behind the beach. Inland, a fertile triangular plain, enclosed by wooded hills to the north, stretches east and west.
10km southwest of Zákynthos Town.

Turtle nesting grounds

A 2km stretch of dunes and beach has been set aside as protected nesting ground for the endangered loggerhead turtles which lay their eggs here each year. Nests are protected by wire enclosures and must not be disturbed. See pages 42–3.
1km east of Laganás, stretching towards Kalamáki.

MONÍ ANAFONÍTRIA (ANAFONITRIA MONASTERY)

A survivor of several quakes, the monastery (it's also a nunnery) has a pretty medieval bell-tower with faded frescos and a cell claimed to have been the refuge of Ágios Dionissos, the island's patron saint.
40km northwest of Zákynthos Town.
Open: daily except during prayer.

ÓRMOS ÁLIKON (ALIKES BAY)

This is the second-best swimming and sunbathing location on Zákynthos after Laganás, and those in search of less crowded beaches may rank it even higher as it is far less developed. It stretches for several kilometres – sandy at the southeast end, pebbly as the bay bends northwestwards. Two low-key resorts, Alikes and Alikanás, are separated by a 2km stretch of lovely yellow sand at the southeast end of the bay.
15 to 20km northwest of Zákynthos Town.

ZÁKYNTHOS TOWN (ZANTE TOWN)

The island's port and capital is a cheerful mixture of post-1953 buildings and a couple of medieval survivors, including a Venetian castle which dominates the town and lends it character.
Northeast coast.

Ágios Nikólaos

The lovely 15th-century church was restored after the 1953 earthquake and is

one of the prettiest in all the Ionian.
Platía Solomoú.
Open: daily.

Kástro (Castle)
The mighty ramparts and turrets of the castle were strong enough to withstand not only the Turks but earthquakes as well. It is one of the island's handful of surviving medieval buildings. On a clear day there is a good view of the mainland.
On the hilltop above the harbour. Open: Tuesday to Sunday 8.30am–2.30 pm. Admission charge.

Moussío Neo-Byzantino (Museum of Neo-Byzantine Art)
Works here include 15th- to 19th-century icons rescued from earthquake-demolished churches and striking paintings from the 17th-century Ionian School. The artists of this movement, fleeing the Turkish conquest of Crete, combined traditional religious themes and Italian Renaissance influences in their painting.
Platía Solomoú. Open: Tuesday to Sunday 8.30am–3pm. Admission charge.

A statue of the poet Dionysius Solomou stands outside the Museum of Neo-Byzantine Art. Exhibits include an icon of St Nicholas (inset)

TURTLES ON THE BRINK

The sweeping sands of the Gulf of Laganás (Kólpos Lagana) are one of a handful of nesting sites of the endangered loggerhead turtle (*Caretta caretta*). Unfortunately, the turtles, which also lay their eggs on beaches in Crete and Kefalloniá, nest on exactly the kind of long, sandy beaches that tourists covet. Mother turtles arrive to lay their eggs in early summer, and the babies hatch two months later. But there are many dangers: females on their way to and from the nesting sites may be injured by speedboats; vehicles driving along the beach compress the sand, making it hard to lay eggs or crushing nests already buried; bright lights from waterside tavernas attract the hatchlings inland, where they die of thirst and exhaustion; sun-loungers crush the sand and the metal poles of parasols can smash buried eggs.

The Greek government has banned night flights from Zákynthos airport, just inland from the bay, and a long stretch of the beach between Laganás and Kalamáki has been set aside as a reserve: vehicles and building are banned and nests are protected. Powerboats are prohibited from travelling at more than six knots in a large sector of the bay, but this ban is sadly often ignored. At least most tour operators urge their clients not to indulge in powered watersports at

Laganás. You should also boycott boatmen who cash in on the turtle craze by offering turtle-spotting cruises. These do more harm than good by harassing mother turtles on their way to and from the beach.

In the last 20 years the number of loggerheads nesting at Laganás has halved. At sea, they are vulnerable to nets, lines and pollution, and since only one hatchling in a thousand survives to lay its own eggs the odds are stacked

Loggerhead turtles have nested here for millions of years, but today their numbers are dwindling

against *Caretta caretta*.

Loggerhead turtles may have laid their eggs at Laganás for 80 million years. It would be tragic if a mere 20 years of tourism were to finish them off.

How you can help:

• No lights or noise on nesting beaches at night

• Don't leave litter on the beach or in the sea

• Don't put up sun-umbrellas in the dry sand where the turtles nest

• Don't try to help the hatchlings reach the sea. Doing it themselves is vital to their development

• Don't disturb any nests you find

• Don't take powerboat rides in the restricted zone of the Laganás Gulf.

Further information: WWF Greece, Asklipiou 14, 10680 Athens (tel: 01 3634 661).

Cruise around Zákynthos

This cruise around Zákynthos offers spectacular coastlines, a view of the island's less accessible beaches, and a glimpse of Zákynthos's mountainous northern neighbour, Keffaloniá, on the horizon.

In early summer the sharp-eyed may spot metre-long loggerhead turtles on their way to the egg-laying beaches (see pages 42–3) and there is always a chance of seeing dolphins too, especially if the sea is particularly calm.

Cold drinks are sold on board and lunch is usually included in the cruise price. Two or three boats leave Zákynthos harbour every morning in high season and tickets are sold by agencies at all the resorts and by tour operator representatives. *The 60km round trip takes about 7 hours, including stops for lunch and swimming.*

Leaving Zákynthos harbour the boat turns north, rounding the headland where the Venetian castle sits, then heads northwest along the line of the island's coast. Akr Tripití (Cape Trypiti), the westernmost point of the Peloponnese mainland, can be seen on the eastern horizon.

1 KÁSTRO (CASTLE OF THE ORSINIS)

Above the harbour at Zákynthos Town stand the battlements of the medieval castle, built by the Orsini family, who ruled several Ionian islands in the Venetian era. The castle is one of the few buildings to survive the 1953 quake, testimony to the skill of its builders.

The boat cruises northwest, with the sands of Tsiliví beach on the port bow and the hills and farmlands of northern Zákynthos above them.

2 ÓRMOS ÁLIKON (ALIKES BAY)

Alikes Bay shelters some of Zákynthos's finest beaches at its southern end.

3 KIANOU SPÍLAIO

The blue-water sea-caves near the
island's northernmost tip are Zákynthos's
most striking natural attraction. A trick
of the light makes the sea in and around
the arched limestone caverns seem
luminously blue. If you stop to snorkel
you will find that underwater swimmers
seem to have been dyed blue too.
*Rounding the northern promontory, the boat
turns west, with the 1,628m peak of Mount
Aínos, the highest point on the Kefallonian
coast, clearly visible to the north.*

4 SMUGGLER'S WRECK

Stranded on a half-moon beach of rough
white sand, hemmed in by sheer
limestone cliffs, is the wreck of a Greek
freighter which went aground in 1982,
carrying an illicit cargo of cigarettes and
liquor destined for Syria. Local tales say
much of the cargo was never recovered.
The picturesque scene has been captured
on a thousand postcards.
*Most cruises stop at Smuggler's Wreck beach
for lunch and swimming before returning to
Zákynthos Town late afternoon.*

Smuggler's Wreck beach (above) and fishing
boats at anchor at Skinari, at the island's tip

Argo-Saronic Islands

*T*he Saronikós Kólpos (Saronic Gulf) lies south of Athens and is sheltered to the north and west by the Isthmus of Corinth and the Attica peninsula. This is the busiest stretch of the Aegean, criss-crossed by millionaires' cruisers, yachts, liners, ferries and merchant vessels.

The ruin-studded shores of the Argolid peninsula divides the eastern Saronic Gulf from the western Argolic Gulf (Kólpos Argolikós) which bites deep into the Peloponnese mainland. The Argo-Saronic is home to four principal holiday islands – Aígina (Aegina), Ýdra (Hydra), Póros and Spétses, plus the two lesser

known isles of Salamína (Salamis) and Agkístri (Angistrion), and many other unvisited rocks.

Only a hop away from Athens and its port of Píreas, these islands are a refuge for city-dwellers as well as holidaymakers. Many better-off Athenians have weekend homes here, and many more take

ARGO-SARONIC ISLANDS

advantage of the fast and frequent ferries and hydrofoils for a day's outing.

Nevertheless, the islands are in many ways closer to the visitor's Greek idyll than many of those in the Aegean's remoter reaches.

Salamína, the closest of the islands to Athens, is historically renowned, for it was in the straits between it and the mainland that the Athenian triremes annihilated the Persian fleet in 480BC. Nowadays, however, it is virtually an industrial and residential suburb of Athens.

There are few vehicles on these islands, and the little harbours with their steep tiers of white shipowners' mansions and villas are very much as first-time visitors to the Greek islands imagine them. They have avoided the kind of holiday invasion which has swamped less prosperous island communities.

Aígina and its satellite Agkístri, in the middle of the Saronic Gulf, are the closest of the group to Athens. Póros, further south, is only a few hundred metres off the Peloponnese coast. Ýdra lies midway between the Saronic and Argolic waters, and Spétses is at the very tip of the Argolid peninsula.

Ýdra's picturesque harbour was once the base of wealthy sea-traders

The Temple of Aphaia, one of the best examples of island temples

AGKÍSTRI

The tiniest of the main Saronic islands, Agkístri has a single sandy beach at Skála, on its north coast. Crowded in the Athenian getaway season, it is quieter than the other isles for the rest of the year, and most of its islanders still live by fishing and farming.
8km west of Aígina.

AÍGINA (AEGINA)

The biggest of the Argo-Saronic isles, Aígina has a fertile hinterland of small farms, a small fishing harbour where tiny boats unload even tinier whitebait, and one busy resort. During the War of Independence (1821–30) Aígina Town was (for a time) the first capital of independent Greece.
25km south of Píreas.

AGÍA MARÍNA

Aígina's main resort, busiest at weekends and in the mid-July to late August Athens holiday season, is on a landlocked bay with a long, but usually crowded, sandy beach.
On the east coast.

Naós Afaía (Temple of Aphaia)

The loveliest and most complete of surviving Greek island temples, with 25 of its 32 tapering columns still standing, built between 480 and 410BC.
9km east of Aígina Town (tel: 0297 32398). Open: Monday to Friday 8.15am–5pm, weekends 8.30am–3pm. Admission charge.

AÍGINA TOWN

Aígina Town's charm lies in its narrow lanes of pinkwashed and whitewashed houses and its quayside cafés overlooking the old-fashioned fishing harbour and ferry port. It's an ideal spot for watching a typical Greek island port – chaotic activity when the ferry arrives, slumbering inactivity between sailings.
On the west coast of the island.

Kolona (Temple of Apollo)

A lofty 8m-high fluted column marks the site of the 6th-century BC Temple of Apollo. Archaeologists have uncovered stretches of walls near by from the same period. A museum displays finds from this and other excavations, including elegant fragments of sculpture.
Immediately north of the town beach, about 750km from the harbour (tel: 0297 22637). Open: Tuesday to Sunday 8.30am–3pm. Admission charge.

PALAIOCHÓRA

This derelict hillside village was Aígina's capital until the 19th century and in its

18th-century heyday boasted around 400 houses and 20-odd churches and chapels. Some of these, from as early as the 13th century, have been restored. Venetian ramparts crown the hill above.
8km east of Aígina Town, on the Agía Marína road.

PÓROS

Tiny Póros is so close to the mainland that you feel you could reach out and touch it – at its closest the Peloponnese is only 256m away.

The island has but one village, also called Póros, and a scattering of shingle beaches This harbour village is on the small peninsula of Sferia, facing the mainland. A narrow isthmus connects Sferia to the hilly, pine-wooded main body of the island, known as Kalavria.
50km south of Píreas.

ASKELI
Askeli is Póros's best beach and has developed into a small but busy holiday resort.
2 to 3km south of Póros Town.

MONÍ ZOODOCHOS PIGI (MONASTERY OF THE SOURCE OF LIFE)
This lovely whitewashed, cloistered building, is dedicated to the Virgin, under one of her many Greek Orthodox guises as the Source of Life. The monastery stands in a grove of tall cypresses and has splendid views of the mainland coast. Below it there is a pleasant small beach for swimming.
4km east of Póros Town. Open: daily. Admission charge.

NAÓS POSSIDHONIA (TEMPLE OF POSEIDON)
The once great 6th-century BC temple has been reduced to a few stone walls and is worth visiting more for the location than for what is left of the structure. In the 18th century it was used as a quarry for marble blocks for the building of a monastery on Ýdra.
8km northeast of Póros Town. Freely accessible.

PÓROS TOWN (CHÓRA)
Cheerful and busy, Póros Town and its white boxy houses cover a beehive-shaped hillock, which is connected by a bridge and causeway to the main part of the island. The streets on and behind the lagoon-like harbour are cluttered with colourful stalls and shops.

Boats shuttle to and from the harbour, taking visitors to beaches around the island or across the strait to the mainland.
West coast, on Sferia peninsula.

Churches in derelict Palaiochóra are still in regular use

Wooden fishing boats are built in the traditional way on Spétses

SPÉTSES (SPETSES)

The furthest of the Argo-Saronic isles from Athens, Spétses is just off the southern tip of the Argolid peninsula. Much of the island is covered with pinewoods planted in the last century. *85km southwest of Píreas.*

SPÉTSES TOWN
Eighteenth- and 19th-century shipowners' mansions are a feature of the chic island capital, a hideaway for the many well-off Athenians who keep second homes here, giving Spétses a much more stylish air than most islands. The town is attractively laid out, with broad squares and avenues.
Northeast coast.

Ágios Nikólaos
The monastery of St Nicholas was the first building in the islands to fly the flag of independent Greece in 1821. Its courtyard is a mosaic of black and white pebbles in typically Spetsiot style.
On Palaio Limani (Old Harbour).
Open: daily.

Moussío Mexis (Mexis Mansion)
The former 18th-century home of Hadziyannis Mexis, one of Spétses's wealthiest merchants, is now a museum dedicated to the great Spetsiot admirals of the 19th century, who played a leading role in the liberation struggle against the Turks.
Behind the Town Hall.
Open: 7am–2.30pm. Admission charge.

Palaio Limani (Old Harbour)
The superb natural anchorage of the old harbour which made Spétses wealthy is now a haven for the opulent yachts of wealthy Athenians.

ÝDRA (HYDRA)

Like a long, thin ship, Ýdra rides at anchor off the south coast of the Argolid peninsula. In the 18th century, at the height of its prosperity, Ýdra's merchant fleet numbered 160 ships and 20,000 people lived here. The only vehicles on the island are two municipal trucks and much of the island is covered by pines.
50km south of Píreas.

ÝDRA TOWN

Ýdra charms new arrivals with a steep façade of tall stone mansions, white houses with pantiled roofs, and a harbourside lined with chic cafés.
Midway along the north coast.

Arkhondiki

Many elegant 18th-century town houses once belonging to the island's great merchant families, have been preserved or restored and some may be visited at certain times.
For visits, enquire at the Dhimotikon (Town Hall) on the waterfront.

KAMINI

Ýdra's most accessible beaches are pebbly strands at Kamini and Kastello.
1,000 to 1,500m west of the harbour.

MANDRÁKI

This is the only sandy beach on Ýdra and features a watersports centre.
3km east of the harbour.

PROFÍTIS ILÍAS AND AGÍA EVPRAXIA

The monastery of Profitis Ilías and the nunnery of Agía Evpraxia face each other on a 500m mountain slope about two hours' steep walk from town, through young pine forests covering the scars of the forest fire of 1985.
2km south of Ýdra Town. Open: daily, except during prayer.

The hillside streets of Póros Town (page 49) are cluttered with colourful stalls and shops

CYCLADES

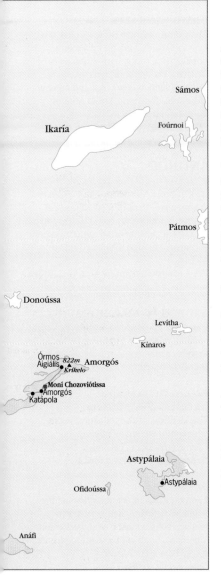

Kykládes (Cyclades)

*L*ying in a scattered circle in the southwest Aegean, the many isles of the Cyclades archipelago are the archetypal Greek islands. Most are small and rocky, and some are no more than dots on the map, though Náxos, the largest of the group, is broad and fertile.

Their white villages and blue-domed chapels are pictured on thousands of postcards, and most of them have at least one fine beach. It comes as no surprise, then, to find that the most popular of the group are among the busiest holiday islands in Greece, and that tourism has wrought dramatic changes. Islands which were peaceful and poor a generation ago are now lively holiday centres.

However, the most popular centres are still outnumbered by close neighbouring isles which see only a trickle of visitors each year. And even on the busiest of islands, you can always find less visited spots.

Among the most popular islands are Mýkonos and Thíra (Santoríni), each with its own international airport; Páros where ferry routes in all directions meet; and Íos, which has become Greece's most popular summer party island. Those less visited, except by Athenian holidaymakers and others in the know, include Folégandros, Sérifos, Síkinos and Sífnos.

Before falling to the Turks in the mid-16th century, the Cyclades formed the Duchy of Náxos, ruled by the Venetian Sanudo dynasty who seized the islands following the Fourth Crusade in 1204.

AMORGÓS

A slender, elongated island, peaceful Amorgós has a delightful hilltop capital (Chóra), uncrowded beaches and a dazzling cliffside monastery. A sheer-sided mountain ridge connects the clusters of settlement and cultivation at either end of the island. Hilltops are often crowned by the round stone towers of medieval windmills, and cobbled hill-paths make Amorgós a fine walker's island.
25km southeast of Náxos.

AMORGÓS TOWN

Amorgós's capital is a classic Cycladic village citadel of whitewashed lanes and archways around a flagstoned central square full of café tables. It sits on a ridge high above the shore with views north and south to neighbouring islands.
Approximately midway along the island's central ridge.

Kástro

The shell of the 13th-century castle of the Venetian Ghisi family crowns the village.
Signposted. Freely accessible.

KATÁPOLA

The western port is a sleepy harbour with a long waterfront which only comes to life with the arrival of the ferry.
4km below Amorgós Town, on the north coast.

MONÍ CHOZOVIOTISSA

The brilliant white walls of this 11th-century monastery cling miraculously to the bare cliff. Founded in 1088 by the Byzantine Emperor, Alexios I Comnenos, its greatest treasure is a miracle-working 11th-century icon of the Virgin, kept in its own gold- and silver-lined chapel.

3km northeast of Amorgós Town, signposted. Open: daily 8am–2pm. Admission charge.

ÓRMOS AIGIÁLIS

The island's eastern port sits on a tiny delta of fertile farmland beneath terraced slopes, rising to the bare 822m peak of Kríkelo. The small village has a long beach of sand and pebbles and there are more secluded coves within walking distance to the east.
10km east of Amorgós Town, on the north coast.

ÁNDROS

Larger, more prosperous, and closer to the mainland than its Cycladic sisters, Ándros hardly seems one of the group at all. It has mostly resisted the temptations of tourism, though it has a couple of small resorts.
13km from the south coast of Évvoia, 35km northeast of Cape Sounion (Akr Soúnio).

ÁNDROS TOWN (CHÓRA)

A modern harbour town, with two large beaches plus some imposing 19th-century sea merchants' mansions.
On the east coast.

Moussío Arkheologiko (Archaeological Museum)

The highlight of the collection is the 4th-century BC statue of Hermes.
Town centre. Open: Tuesday to Sunday 8.30am–3pm. Admission charge.

BATSÍ

Ándros's main resort has a fine sandy beach, crowded in high season with package holidaymakers and weekending Athenians, lined with a modern strip of hotels, bars and tavernas.
12km west of Ándros Town.

The hillside monastery of Panachrántou has wonderful views, but there are few monks to enjoy them

MONÍ PANACHRÁNTOU (PANACHRANTOS MONASTERY)

The 10th-century fortress monastery is impressive but almost deserted, clinging to grim grey and red cliffs.

4km southwest of Ándros Town. Open: daily, daylight hours.

ANTÍPAROS

See page 64.

ASTYPÁLAIA

Geographically and culturally one of the Cyclades, Astypálaia was lumped in with the Dodecanese islands (see pages 84–5) by an accident of history. When international arbitrators were brokering the independence of Greece from Turkey (1832) they drew the line west of the island, and it remained under foreign rule until 1947.

The island is barren and rocky, almost cut in two by deep bays. The isthmus between them is just wide enough for the road to pass. Though remote, Astypálaia

is popular with fashionable Athenians and its only village, Astypálaia Town, is surprisingly stylish.

ASTYPÁLAIA TOWN (CHÓRA)

The chic island capital is striking even by Cycladic standards. Its white houses with two or three storeys and pretty painted shutters combine influences from its western sisters and from the islands further east. They cover the hilltop above a perfect natural harbour.

Northwest Astypálaia.

Kástro

The dilapidated Venetian-Turkish castle has an endearingly slapdash appearance. Its walls are cobbled together from slabs and blocks looted from earlier buildings, and it enjoys panoramic views to the empty horizons around the island.

On the highest point of the village. Freely accessible.

DÍLOS

See pages 74–5.

FOLÉGANDROS

Tall and craggy, Folégandros looks like a stone ship steaming towards the mainland. Seemingly barren slopes, covered with terraces where barley and olives thrive, are testimony to centuries of hard peasant labour. The northeast coast of the island is dominated by sheer cliffs, while the more sheltered southwest side boasts a handful of small undeveloped beaches.

The neighbouring isles of Thíra (Santoríni), Íos and Síkinos can be seen on the horizon, and on a clear day islanders claim that they can see Crete, more than 100km to the south.
50km southwest of Náxos.

Traditional windmill on Íos, with thatched roof and canvas sails

FOLÉGANDROS TOWN (CHÓRA)

One of the loveliest Cycladic villages, Folégandros Town perches high above the sea among terraced hills and is built around the Piatsa, a flagstoned central square. From the archway off the south side of the square you enter the picturesque, dazzling white, fortress-like warren of archways and houses known as the Kástro.
In the centre of the island.

KHRISSOSPILIA

A startling blue sea cavern which bores into the cliffs of the north coast.
1km southeast of Folégandros Town, accessible only by boat from Karavostásis, the island's port, 3km southeast of Folégandros Town.

ÍOS

Greece's supreme party island throbs to a summer beat from June to the end of August, when it attracts young ravers from all over the world who pack its bars, beaches and discos. It is quieter out of season, when it offers non-ravers a choice of fine sandy beaches on each coast.
25km south of Náxos.

ÁGIOS THEODÓTIS

This long sandy stretch on the east coast of the island, overlooked by the ruins of a Venetian fort is the less crowded of Íos's two easy-access beaches.
10km east of Íos Town.

ÍOS TOWN (CHÓRA)

Íos's Chóra conforms to Cycladic style, but dozens of bars, discos and restaurants – virtually every building is now one or the other – have obliterated the local culture.
On a hilltop on the island's west coast.

Órmos Íou (Yialos)

Íos Town's harbour annex, immediately below the village, is on a fiord-like bay with its own beach where ferries call frequently.
1km west of Íos Town.

MYLOPÓTAMOS

The closest beach to Íos Town and the most crowded despite its huge size, southwest-facing Mylopótamos is a solid mass of sunbathing bodies by day and beach slumberers by night.
1km from Íos Town.

ÓRMOS MANGANÁRI

The least accessible of Íos's major beaches, Manganári's six small silvery sand strips face south and are reached by boat from Yialos.
12km southeast of Íos Town.

PLAKATOS ('HOMER'S TOMB')

Íos is one of many islands claiming a link with the author of the *Iliad* and the *Odyssey*. Beware, however, that the remnants of the tomb at the site of ancient Plakatos are poorly signposted, difficult to reach and are probably Byzantine.
Near the north tip of the island, 9km northeast of Íos Town. Freely accessible.

KÉA (TZEA)

Close to the mainland, Kéa is busy with Athenian weekenders in July and August but sees few foreigners and few visitors of any kind for much of the year. An egg-shaped isle with a hilly, wooded interior, it has little in common with its Cycladic neighbours.
20km east of Lávrio on the mainland, 90km northwest of Náxos.

Centuries of labour went into landscapes like this terraced hillside

KÉA TOWN (IOULIDHA)

The main village, set in a pretty inland valley, is a mix of traditional red-tiled homes and newer buildings.
North central Kéa.

Arkheologiko Moussío (Archaeological Museum)

Collection of discoveries from four ancient Kean sites.
Platía Mousiou. Open: Tuesday to Sunday 8.30am–3pm. Admission charge.

Kástro

A tumbledown castle built by the Venetians, using remnants of an ancient sanctuary of Apollo.
1km from the village centre, signposted. Freely accessible.

Lion of Kéa

This magnificent 3m-high stone lion was carved from the hillside in the 6th century BC.
2km northeast of the centre. Freely accessible.

KÍMOLOS

This tiny satellite of Mílos (see below) is one of the Aegean's great escapes, with virtually no tourism.
1.5km from Mílos.

KÍMOLOS TOWN (CHÓRA)
The island's main village is a clutter of white hillside houses backed by six windmills.
In the middle of the island, 1km from Psáthi.

PALAIÓKASTRO
The battlements of a ruined Venetian fortress surround the island's oldest church, the whitewashed Hristos chapel.
2km northwest of Kímolos Town. Freely accessible.

KÝTHNOS

Most visitors bypass gentle Kýthnos – the first stop on the ferry route from Píreas to the western Cyclades – en route to better-known isles further south, and it is hard to argue that they are missing much.

Kýthnos has little to offer by way of beaches, or sightseeing and its landscapes are less dramatic than many of its neighbours.

Few visitors disembark at the peaceful island of Kýthnos

DRYOPÍDA
Stucco-walled homes with red-tiled roofs make this farming village – the island's capital in medieval times – look more Italian than Cycladic.
5km south of Kýthnos Town.

Spíli Katafigi (Cave of Refuge)
In the middle of the village, the locally famous cave once provided islanders with shelter against pirate raids.
Freely accessible.

KÉFALOS (AKR KÉFALOS)
The ruins of a medieval Venetian castle crown the north-facing headland.
North tip of the island, 7km from Kýthnos Town. Freely accessible.

KÝTHNOS TOWN (CHÓRA)
The remaining traditional buildings of the village are dwarfed by new construction.
Centre of the island.

Metamórphosis (Church of the Transfiguration)
An interesting 17th-century church.
Village centre. Open: daily. Free admission.

MÍLOS

Mílos's weirdly sculpted landscapes are part of its appeal, not only for visitors but for the earliest neolithic islanders, who valued the obsidian found in its volcanic soil. The island's soft rock is easily eroded by wind and water, and Mílos's coasts are marked by twisted stone formations and

offshore islets carved by the sea. The island has also been shaped by human hand and quarrying for cement and china-clay continues today. Mílos is somewhat doughnut-shaped, with a wide, almost landlocked bay which takes a deep bite out of its north coast, and is less mountainous than most of the Cyclades.
161km south of Píreas.

ADÁMAS
Ferries call at the functional harbour at Adámas, on the east shore of the Gulf of Mílos.
5km from Mílos Town.

MÍLOS TOWN (CHÓRA)
The main island village is half-traditional, half-modern, with an assortment of sights, of which the ruins of the ancient city are the most worthwhile.
On the northern headland of the Gulf of Mílos.

Arkheologiko Moussío (Archaeological Museum) and ancient Mílos
Traces of the ancient city including the remains of the 5th-century BC acropolis, an intact Roman theatre, and 3rd-century AD Christian tombs can be seen. The museum collection includes neolithic earthenware and a replica of the Venus de Milo.
500km west/downhill from the village centre. Open: museum and site, Tuesday to Sunday 8.30am–3pm. Admission charge for both.

Kástro (Castle)
The small Venetian citadel is well preserved.
Hilltop site, 500m from village atop a cobbled stair. Freely accessible.

Laografiko Moussío (Folklore Museum)
Costumes, furniture and decorative items from everyday island life.
Village centre. Open: Tuesday to Saturday 10am–1pm and 6pm–8pm. Admission charge.

SPÍLIA (CAVES)
Mílos's volcanic shores have been hollowed out by the waves, and its coasts are pierced by several spectacular caverns, used in medieval years by piratical islanders. There are boat trips to the caves from Adámas.

Kleftikó (Robber's Caves)
White chalk cliffs and pinnacles, honeycombed with pirate caves.
South coast.

Papafranga (French Priest's Cave)
Three caves big enough to shelter boats tunnel into the cliffside.
South coast.

Sikia (Emerald Cave)
A trick of the light makes the water glow green here.
Near the southwest point of the island.

Souvenirs from Mílos: copies of the Venus de Milo

Whitewashed walls and narrow alleys are typical of Mýkonos

MÝKONOS

Superb sandy beaches, a stunningly attractive main town (for once at sea-level instead of high above) and just offshore one of classical Greece's most fascinating ancient temple sites make for a potent combination which attracts a very wide clientele. Wealthy Greek and expatriate villa owners rub shoulders with package holidaymakers (who fly direct to the island), cruise ship passengers who come ashore for a day shopping and sightseeing, and a large gay community.

The first Aegean island to attract tourists in numbers, (more than 750,000 visitors a year) Mýkonos is the most popular and best-known of the Cyclades, with a worldwide reputation. Mýkonos nightlife is legendary and its holiday season is much longer than that of its neighbours, with a hard core of long-stay visitors who arrive early in the season and

Whitewashed walls and narrow alleys are typical of Mýkonos

leave late. The island's famous beaches are strung along the south coast, sheltered from northerly winds and conveniently accessible by a constant daytime shuttle of small boats.

Dílos, the finest ancient location in the Cyclades, is included in this section as it is most easily accessible from Mýkonos and has no accommodation. *25km north of Náxos.*

DÍLOS (DELOS)

Dílos was sacred to the god Apollo and in the 5th century BC was the hub of the Delian League, a federation of islands dominated by Athens. Many of its temples were built during this era, others during the height of its prosperity as the most important Aegean port in the early Roman era (2nd and 1st centuries BC). For full description of the site see pages 74–5.
10km southwest of Mýkonos Town.

Arkheologiko Moussío (Archaeological Museum)

A fine collection of sculptures from the sanctuary of Artemis and the Temple of Athena and smaller Hellenistic finds of bronze, gold and ivory.
Museum and site open: Tuesday to Sunday 8.30am–3pm. Admission charge.
Boats leave Mýkonos Town daily at 8.30am, returning around 1pm.

MÝKONOS TOWN (CHÓRA)

Alefkandhra (Little Venice), is the most picturesque part of town, with brightly painted wooden balconies dangling over the sea from the high white walls of Venetian town houses.
400m southwest of the harbour.

Arkheologiko Moussío (Archaeological Museum)

Decorated vases and other finds from sites on Dílos and the uninhabited islet of Ríneia.

South end of Andhronikou, signposted. Open: Tuesday to Sunday 8.30am–3pm. Admission charge.

Laografiko Moussío (Folk Museum)

A glimpse of old Mýkonos; a 19th-century island home with traditionally decorated and furnished interiors.

On the harbour, near Paraportiani church. Open: Monday to Saturday 5.30–8.30pm, Sunday 6.30–8.30pm. Free admission.

Mílos Boni (Boni Windmill)

The much-photographed, whitewashed 16th-century windmill is one of the most evocative symbols of Mýkonos.

Leonidiou Boni, 300m east of harbour. Open: daily 4pm–8pm, July to September.

PARADISSI (PARADISE BEACH)

The most popular of Mýkonos's beaches, this half-moon of fine sand on a sheltered bay with plenty of good tavernas is favoured by nude sunbathers.

6km southeast of Mýkonos Town.

PLATÝS GIALÓS

The closest to Mýkonos Town, and the busiest and most developed of the islands beaches with lots of hotels and sun-loungers squeezed into its sandy strip. Platýs Gialós is on the sheltered west side of a south facing bay, looking across to Psarou beach on the east shore.

4km south of Mýkonos Town.

PLINDIRI ('SUPER PARADISE')

This is Mýkonos's best beach by far.

10km southeast of Mýkonos.

Vividly painted woodwork brightens Alefkandhra, nicknamed Little Venice

NÁXOS

Varied landscapes and a rich trove of ancient and medieval finds make Náxos, the largest of the Cyclades, one of the most attractive islands in the group. Despite an air link to Athens its excellent beaches and a fascinating little capital, the impact of tourism is visibly less here than on its nearest large neighbours, Páros and Mýkonos, and there is room for more adventurous visitors to escape to empty beaches and a choppy landscape of farming valleys and high peaks.

Náxos is pear-shaped and measures some 35km from north to south. A steep ridge of peaks, rising to the 1001m high Náxos-Zéfs, divides the barren and almost uninhabited east from the more populous and fertile west. Here, the coastal plain and inland pockets of rich soil are covered with lemon, orange and olive groves, wheat, barley and potato fields, and vineyards which make up some of the best wines in the islands.

APÓLLON (KOUROS OF APOLLO)

Apóllon is a quiet, pretty fishing village with a minute harbour and small beach. The reclining figure of a naked youth (*kouros*) was carved from the marble hillside some time in the 7th century BC, but for some reason was never finished.
Beside the ancient marble quarry, above the Chóra road, 33km northeast of Náxos Town. Freely accessible.

CHALKÍ

A prosperous farming village set in the lovely pastoral landscape of the Tragea valley, covered with lemon and olive-groves, on the slopes of Náxos-Zéfs.
17km east of Náxos Town.

Panayia Protothronos (Church of the Virgin)

Built over some 300 years of Byzantine rule (9th–13th centuries), the charming parish church has colourful frescos.
Main street. Open: daily (if locked enquire at community office on main street).

Pirgos Frangopoulo (Frangopoulos Tower)

A well-preserved mansion tower house.
Main street; closed.

NÁXOS TOWN (CHÓRA)

The island capital is a prosperous town. Its architecture blends Cyclades cubism and faded medieval Venetian elegance, and courtyards filled with scented jasmine and crimson geraniums makes its inner maze of alleys less austere than the whitewashed purity of Mýkonos or Thíra (Santorini). It became the capital of the medieval Duchy of Náxos in 1207 when the Venetian Marco Sanudo seized the island, and was ruled by his descendants for more than five centuries until its conquest by the Turkish pirate Barbarossa in 1566.

Arkheologiko Moussío (Archaeological Museum)

An outstanding collection of statues, Cycladic-era ceramics and idols, well laid-out and explained, housed in a 17th-century school.
Within the kástro. Open: Tuesday to Sunday 8.30am–3pm. Admission charge.

Kástro (Castle of the Sanudos)

The pretty 13th-century castle is much less grim than its counterparts elsewhere. The ramparts are whitewashed and blend with the surrounding local houses, while the grand town houses within, built around inner courtyards, are still the private homes of Naxiot bluebloods who claim descent from the Venetian nobility. Within the walls too are the Archaeological Museum (see opposite) and cathedral (see below).

Village centre; follow Odós Apolonos uphill to main gate, flanked by a huge tower. Freely accessible.

Mitropoli (Cathedral)

The 13th-century cathedral, built by the first Sanudo, has a fine Byzantine icon of the Virgin and Ioannis Prodhromos (John the Baptist).

Within the kástro. Open: daily. Free admission.

Temple of Apollo Gateway

The towering marble gateway, all that remains of the grand 6th-century BC Temple of Apollo, is Náxos Town's most striking landmark. Local people believed it to be the portal of the palace of Ariadne, the lover of the legendary hero Theseus, who was abandoned by him on Náxos.

On Palatia headland, 500m north of the centre.

The gateway of the Temple of Apollo, on the Palatia headland

PYRGOS VELÓNIA (BELLONIA TOWER)

This medieval tower house belonged to the Roman Catholic bishops of the island.

6km southeast of Náxos Town. Not normally open to visitors.

PÁROS

Páros has a big reputation, with excellent sandy beaches, an island capital which combines Cycladic charm with noisy summer nightlife, and a clutch of man-made and natural attractions.

Two fine natural anchorages on the west and north coasts shelter the two main villages, and the roughly circular island rises to the 771m peak of Profitis Ilías, summit of the Óros Márpissa massif which dominates the hinterland.

The satellite island of Antíparos, only minutes away by boat from its bigger sister, is also dealt with here.
Páros is 5km west of Náxos.

ANTÍPAROS

There are two reasons for a trip to Antíparos. One is to visit its beaches – crowded in July and August – and the other is to see its enormous limestone cave. The only village is on the north tip.
1km southwest of Páros.

Ágios Geórgios

The best and least busy of the Antíparos beaches, a scattering of sandy coves facing southwest.
12km south of Antíparos village.

Spílaio Stalaktitón (Cave)

The great cavern is adorned with weirdly shaped rock formations and extends 90m into the hillside.
7km south of Antíparos village, signposted. Open: daily 9am–2pm. Admission charge.

CHRYSÍ AKTÍ (GOLDEN BEACH)

The best of Páros's sandy beaches, with several smaller coves and beaches to either side.
15km southeast of Páros Town.

LATOMIA MARMÁRON (MARBLE QUARRIES)

Three ancient quarry tunnels, the earliest dating from Classical times, plunge deep into the hillside. Páros was famed for its pure white marble from ancient times into the mid-19th century, when the deposits were worked out.
6km east of Páros Town.

NÁOUSA

The island's second largest settlement, where a one-time fishing village has

Náousa is a cheerful blend of fishing village and holiday resort

mushroomed into a mid-sized resort with small beaches to either side of a north-facing natural harbour.
On the island's north coast.

Pirgos (Tower)
A small stone keep of the Duchy of Náxos, built to guard the harbour.
On the harbour. Freely accessible.

PÁROS TOWN (CHÓRA)
Páros, the island capital, has one of the busiest harbours in the Cyclades, with ferries calling constantly day and night. Its 1.5km esplanade is lined with cafés, bars and restaurants, which at night compete to see which can generate the brightest lights and the loudest music.

Arkheologiko Moussío (Archaeological Museum)
This small collection includes pottery and marble fragments and a 6th-century BC statue of Athena Nike.
Next to Panagia Ekatotapyliani. Open: Tuesday to Sunday 8.30am–3pm. Admission charge.

Kástro (Castle)
This ruined 13th-century Venetian castle incorporates columns and marble blocks from an ancient temple which stood on the same site.
Northern promontory of the bay, 1km from Páros Town centre.

Panagia Ekatotapyliani (Katapoliani/Our Lady of the Hundred Doors)
The original Byzantine church dates from the 6th century, with some 10th-century additions. Its chapel of Ágios

Nikólaos incorporates columns from an earlier Hellenistic temple.
Off Manto Mavrogenous. Open: 8am–midday and 5pm–8pm. Admission free.

PETALOÚDES (VALLEY OF THE BUTTERFLIES)
The Valley of the Butterflies is undoubtredly the island's most charming and colourful attraction. Lemon and apricot trees are grown on both sides of the valley, sheltering vast swarms of scarlet-winged tiger moths which fly up in an explosion of colour. Visit in spring or early summer for the best display.
7km south of Páros Town. Open: daily, daylight hours. Admission charge.

Gleaming chandeliers and wax tapers adorn the Church of Our Lady of the Hundred Doors

THÍRA (SANTORÍNI)

The view of Thíra (Santoríni) from a
ferry pulling into its cliff-ringed bay is
unforgettable. Sheer cliffs in layers of red,
white and greenish-grey volcanic rock
encircle a huge, sea-filled caldera (crater)
which plunges to an enormous depth and
is encircled by Thíra (Santoríni) and its
smaller neighbours, Thirasía and
Aspronísi. Two tiny, still-active volcanic
islets smoulder in the centre of the caldera.

Shaped like a broken circle, the island
was formed by a huge volcanic explosion
*c*1450 BC which blew out its centre leaving
the present huge caldera. Many
archaeologists believe the explosion and
the huge tidal wave it created may have
been the nemesis of the Crete-based
Minoan civilisation which collapsed at
about the same time. (Minoan and
Mycenaean sites have also been excavated
on Santoríni.) In more recent times the
island was also an important medieval
possession of the Dukes of Náxos.

Santoríni's main town,Thíra, is a line
of white battlements along the crater rim.
South of it, the rolling hills rise a little
further to the walls of Pýrgos, a half-
deserted fortress-village. To the east, the
island shelves seaward in a series of
terraced tomato fields and vineyards
before reaching the sea at the black-sand
beaches, Kamári and Périssa on
Santoríni's east coast. A crescent ridge
running from Pýrgos to the east coast
divides the island in two and an ancient
city (see Akrotíri, below) once sat atop its
seaward end.
50km south of Náxos.

AKROTÍRI (AKROTIRI ARCHAEOLOGICAL SITE)

The well-preserved houses and streets of
this 'Greek Pompeii', smothered by the
great eruption, have been excavated since
1935, unearthing graceful 3,500-year-old
frescos which demonstrate the
connection with the Minoan civilisation.
Some minor finds from the site are
displayed in the Thíra Archaeological
Museum (see opposite).
*South coast of southern cape of the island,
18km south of Thíra (tel: 0286 81366).
Open: Tuesday to Sunday 8.30am–3pm.
Admission charge.*

KAMÁRI

Santoríni's biggest resort, on a long,
east-facing beach of black sand which
becomes uncomfortably hot in the
summer sun.
12km southeast of Thíra.

Arkhea Thíra (Ancient Thíra)

Scant remains possibly dating from a
6th-century BC–5th century AD
settlement include foundations of an
ancient agora and a theatre.
*On top of the Mesavouno headland 2km
south of Kamári and 320m above it.
Open: Tuesday to Saturday 8am–3pm.
Admission charge.*

OÍA

This dazzlingly pretty clifftop village
commands huge views, both across the
northern and western horizon, and south
to Thíra and Akrotíri. It was badly
shaken by a minor eruption and earth
tremors in 1956 and remained almost
deserted until the 1980s when restoration
began.

Many of its houses have typical Thíra
(Santoríni) barrel-vaulted roofs (to
withstand earth tremors) and some have
rooms burrowed deep into the soft
volcanic rock. A few have been converted
into characterful guesthouses (see
pages 176–7).

There is a small beach, immediately below the village reached by a steep stair cut into the rock.
8km north of Thíra.

THÍRA TOWN (CHÓRA)

Thíra's geometric buildings form a whitewashed parapet atop 270m-high sea-cliffs. Visitors arriving by sea reach the clifftop town either by donkey, up some 600 breathtaking steps, or by a dizzying cable-car ride from the harbour. There are tiny blue-domed churches at every corner but they are outnumbered by fast-food cafés and expensive jewellers. Thíra is just too photogenic to have escaped mass-market tourism, and like Mýkonos (pages 60–1) has been welcoming visitors since the early 1960s.

Arkheologiko Moussío (Archaeological Museum)

A fine collection spanning two millennia, from the Minoan era to the Roman period.
Ipapantis Street. Open: Tuesday to Sunday 8am–3pm. Admission charge.

Above: multicoloured cliffs of soft volcanic rock loom over the harbour at Amoudi
Below: Oía, reborn as a holiday village

VOLCANOES AND VAMPIRES

Looking over the huge sea-filled crater of Thíra (Santoríni) you can see two jagged black islets in its centre. These are the Kaméni, the 'burnt islands', and you can visit them on a boat excursion from the main island.

Palaia Kaméni, the older of the pair, has been there since the 2nd century BC, when it astonished the Greek world by emerging from the sea in a matter of weeks – proof to the ancients of the power of Poseidon, god of the sea and of earthquakes.

Néa Kaméni, the bigger of the two, made its appearance between AD1707–11. It trebled in size during another eruption in 1866–7 and still shows some signs of activity, with a reek of sulphur from a pool of hot, bubbling mud.

It may be because of this whiff of brimstone that the Kaméni and Thíra (Santoríni) are said to be haunted by vampires – not the Dracula variety but the less substantial Greek kind, wandering spirits which moan and wail at night and are also said to inhabit the deserted hills and canyons of Sfakiá, in southwest Crete. The garlands of wildflowers that islanders gather on 1 May and hang above their doors for the rest of the year bring blessings on the home and keep such evil spirits from crossing the threshold.

Many archaeologists now believe that the explosion which blew the island apart some 3,500 years ago may also have destroyed the thriving Minoan civilisation which dominated the Aegean at that time.

With its capital at Knosós on Crete, the Minoan empire included colonies on Thíra (Santoríni) and other Cycladic islands, but around the time of the Thíra (Santoríni) eruption it collapsed suddenly and inexplicably. The eruption, it is now believed, would have sent huge waves in all directions, destroying ports and cities throughout the Aegean and smothering crops and fields under centimetres of poisonous ash.

As a comparison, when the

A demonic stretch of brimstone hangs over the Néa Kaméni crater

Indonesian island of Krakatoa (Krakatau) exploded in 1883, it raised 15 to 30m-high tidal waves and damaged buildings more than 160km away. It is thought that the Thíra explosion was even bigger than Krakatoa and as Knosós, on Crete, is only half that distance from Santoríni, so the damage to the city, its surrounding lands and to other Minoan settlements would have been extensive.

This 'big bang' theory may not wholly account for the disappearance of the powerful Minoan empire from the Aegean stage, but the timing is persuasive. By the 15th century BC the Minoans were no longer a great power, and Mycenaean settlers from the mainland had moved in to take over the islands they once controlled.

SÉRIFOS

Sérifos is how many people picture all the Greek islands. White houses, churches and a miniature castle all cling precariously to a crag some 2km inland from a perfect natural harbour on a shallow sandy bay. Around the bay square houses splashed with purple and scarlet flowers clutter the hillside, where clumps of greenery cling to the scree and boulder slopes of rocky ravines.
131km southeast of Píreas.

LIVÁDI

Sérifos's port is a cheerful, house-proud assortment of mostly modern, well-kept homes, tavernas and small hotels, enhanced by its bayside location and mountain backdrop. A tiny fertile delta of green farmland and pink oleander-lined creeks extends behind the village.

The tree-lined beach south of the village is not the island's best: there are much better small sandy beaches 10 to 30 minutes' walk away, beyond the headland west of the harbour.
2km southeast of Sérifos Town.

MEGA LIVÁDI

The west-facing beach is the remotest and least-visited large beach on the island.
8km southwest of Sérifos Town.

MONÍ TAXIARCHÓN (MONASTERY OF THE ARCHANGEL MICHAEL)

The 16th-century monastery is often deserted, with a single guardian monk sporadically in residence. There are some minor frescos within, but the visit is worth making as much for the walk through serene hill landscapes as for the destination.
2km northwest of Kállitsos village, 5km north of Sérifos Town, access on foot from Kállitsos, sketchily signposted. Open: irregular hours. Enquire at Sérifos Town community office or at Kállitsos.

PSILÍ ÁMMOS

Serifos's best beach, with a lovely crescent of white sand facing east.
4km north of Livádi, access on foot or by boat.

SÉRIFOS TOWN (CHÓRA)

Sérifos Town is built around and within the walls of a Venetian castle, which is virtually absorbed into the buildings around it. Unlike some Chóras, therefore, it does not stand in splendid isolation, but is just another part of the

Sérifos Town on its inland hilltop overlooks Livádi harbour

pleasant jumble of old stones and whitewashed walls.
2km from east coast.

SÍFNOS

A fertile, pretty island rising steeply from the sea, Sífnos is patchworked with fields and pastureland, criss-crossed with donkey-tracks marked out by dry-stone walls, and dotted with white hill-villages.
136km south of Píreas.

APOLLÓNIA (CHÓRA)
Three characterful hamlets – Artemón, Kamáres and Kataváti, originally about 750m from each other – have blended into a single jumble of whitewashed houses, church-towers, and small café-cluttered squares.
Centre of the island.

Ágios Spiridon (Church of St Spiridon)
The island's main church, built and added to over several centuries, is a fine example of the Sifniot taste for multi-coloured religious architecture, painted in gaudy shades.
On Stylianou Prokhou, the main street.

Laografiko Moussío (Folk Museum)
Beautiful island lace and embroidery, traditional Sifniot costume, and a rusting collection of lethal weaponry.
On the central square at Kamáres. Open: daily 10am–1pm and 6pm–9pm. Admission charge.

KÁSTRO
This medieval Venetian stronghold occupies the finest natural fortress on Sífnos, a sea-crag guarded on three sides. Its characterful alleys, archways and two-storey houses lean tiredly on each other

Apollónia church tower is a blend of Greek and Italianate styles

and have a strong Venetian flavour.
East coast, 4km east of Apóllonia.

Arkheologiko Moussío (Archaeological Museum)
Small collection of finds from the ancient site.
Pano Kástro. Open: Tuesday to Sunday 8.30am–3pm. Admission charge. 3km east of Apóllonia, on the coast.

MONÍ CHRYSOPIGÍ (CHRISSOPIYI MONASTERY)
The picturesque 17th-century monastery, located on a promontory on the east coast, is one of the island's tourism symbols. It is deconsecrated, and you can stay in one of the monks' cells in summer.
6km southeast of Apóllonia (tel: 0284 31225). Open: daylight hours.

SÍKINOS

Tiny, rocky Síkinos is for Greek island purists. It has a high fortress village, a port with a small beach, a few other small beaches around its rocky coasts, and two minor sights.
25km southwest of Náxos.

ALOPRÓNOIA (SKALA)
The port of call for inter-island ferries and yachts; also boasts a small beach.
Southeast coast.

EPISKOPÍ ('TEMPLE OF APOLLO')
A Hellenistic building, perhaps a temple or mausoleum, transformed into a church in the 7th century.
5km southwest of Kástro.

MONÍ ZOODÓCHOU PIGÍS (MONASTERY OF THE SPRING OF LIFE)
A deserted monastery with fine views over the island and its neighbours.
750m above Kástro.

SÍKINOS TOWN (CHÓRA)
Two medieval villages on the rocky spine of the island have merged into one, around a square of fortified medieval houses.
4km from Aloprónia.

SÝROS

One of the most populous islands with 20,000 inhabitants, Sýros is fertile on its west side, barren on its eastern coast, and blessed with the southern Aegean's finest deepwater anchorage.
40km northwest of Náxos.

ERMOÚPOLI
Ermoúpoli, Sýros's capital, is no dinky village but a thriving town of 15,000 folk, and its grandiose town architecture and neo-classical public buildings date from the first half of the 19th century, when it was newly independent Greece's most prosperous city. And it wasn't until

The church of St Nicholas overlooks the busy harbour at Ermoúpoli the completion of the Corinth Canal in 1893 that it was eclipsed by Píreas, the port of Athens.

The lower part of town, between the harbour and gracious main square, Platía Miaoúlis, was laid out in the island's heyday. Above it, on two hills, Áno Sýros to the west and Vrondado to the east, are the town's contrasting medieval quarters. Áno Sýros is a labyrinthine collection of alleys and arches with a scattering of Catholic churches dating from the Venetian era, while Vrondado is the town's Orthodox quarter.

Anastasi

The grand domed Orthodox church was built to rival neighbouring Ágios Geórgios.
At top of Vrondado, 1km north of Platía Miaoúlis. Open: irregular hours. Enquire at town tourist office, Platía Vardhaka.

Arkheologiko Moussío (Archaeological Museum)

Finds from Sýros and nearby islands.
West side of the Town Hall, signposted. Open: Tuesday to Sunday 8.30am–3pm. Admission charge.

Ágios Geórgios (Cathedral of St George)

The Roman Catholic cathedral is built in the Venetian style.
On top of Áno Sýros, 1km from Platía Miaoúlis. Open: daily. Admission free.

Moní Kapoutsino (Capuchin Monastery of St John)

Built in 1535, the monastery survived the Turkish era under French protection.
100m downhill from Ágios Geórgios. Open: daily. Admission free.

FOÍNIKAS/POSEIDONÍA

Sýros's main beach resort, where two villages at either end of a pebble-and-sand bay which faces west have merged.
11km southwest of Ermoúpoli.

TÍNOS

Tínos is the national contemporary shrine of the Greek Orthodox religion. Its tradition as the 'Lourdes of the Aegean' began in 1822 when a sacred icon was revealed in a dream to the nun later beatified as Agía Pelagía. The island is also renowned for its picturesque, geometrically patterned dovecotes which date from Venetian times.
65km northwest of Náxos.

TÍNOS TOWN (CHÓRA)

Modern and unassuming, the town's main attraction is the famous, imposing, white-marble church housing the sacred icon (see below).
Southwest coast.

Arkheologiko Moussío (Archaeological Museum)

This is housed within the church complex and displays discoveries from sites on the island, most strikingly an enormous 7th century BC *pithos* (storage jar).
Leoforos Megalochoris. Open: Tuesday to Sunday 8.30am–3pm. Admission charge.

Panagía Evangelistría (Church of the Annunciation)

Built in 1822 to house the newly discovered icon with its healing powers, this huge fortress-like church complex is the venue of two annual pilgrimages, on 25 March and 15 August.
Leoforos Megalochoris. Open: daily 8.30am–8.30pm. Admission free.

Cruise to Dílos (Delos)

In ancient times Dílos was a sacred and political centre and an important commercial port, and today its outstanding temple sites are among the most striking in Greece.

The best way to visit them is by boat from Mýkonos. These depart daily around 8.30–9am, returning from Dílos at around 1pm. *The crossing takes approximately 30 minutes each way, leaving about 3 hours to explore the ruins.*

Leaving Mýkonos harbour you have a view of the colourful balconies of Alefkandhra ('Little Venice') overhanging the sea. The boat turns south, passing through the narrows between Dílos and the neighbouring islet Ríneia before arriving at Dílos's harbour. There is a combined admission charge for site and museum.

At the landward end of the pier turn north and enter the sanctuary district via the Sacred Way, where the bases of the statues which lined this wide access path can be seen, after 100m this leads to the three worn steps which are the remains of the Propylaia, the great gate.

1 HIERON (SANCTUARY OF APOLLO)

To the left of the Propylaia are the traces of the 6th-century BC Stoa (covered walk) of the Naxiots; on the right are the rectangular foundations of the 7th-century BC temple known as the House of the Naxiots.

The heart of the sanctuary comprises traces of three temples of Apollo, around which are the column-bases and foundations of three smaller religious buildings.

Walk 400m north, and leave the sanctuary via the walls of the 6th-century BC Temple of Leto and the Agorá of the Italians on your right.

2 LION DISTRICT

The row of five stone lions sculpted in marble from Náxos during the 6th–7th century BC are the best-known symbol of Dílos. Originally there were many more. To the east is the site of the Sacred Lake (drained in 1924 to prevent malaria) where the swans dedicated to Apollo once swam.

Turn right, around the site of the lake, and head back south 350m to the museum, on your left as you walk south.

3 MUSEUM

The museum collection includes statues of male and female youths from the Sanctuary of Artemis, 5th-century classical art, Hellenistic sculptures and some delightful small bronze figures and ivory carvings.

Leaving the museum, continue south 500m to the lower slopes of Mount Kýnthos, Dílos's highest point. (Allow 45 minutes for ascent and descent.)

Multi-tiered marble theatre seats date from the Hellenistic era

4 MOUNT KÝNTHOS (ÓROS KÝNTHOS)

At the foot of the hill is the Terrace of the Foreign Gods, where once stood statues of Syrian and Egyptian deities.

After 200m pass on your right the Sacred Cave, a cleft in the rock which was sacred to Herakles (Hercules) and had massive granite doors.

Descending Mount Kýnthos, walk west 100m to the 2nd-century BC Theatre District.

5 THEATRE DISTRICT

On your right, the courtyard of the House of the Dolphins features a superb floor mosaic of dolphins, which were sacred to Apollo. Opposite, the restored two-storey House of the Masks is one of the highlights of Dílos, with more splendid mosaics.

Finally, pass the well-preserved marble tiers of the Hellenistic theatre, the House of the Trident, the House of Cleopatra (not connected with the famous Egyptian queen!), the beautiful panther mosaics of the House of Dionysos and return to the harbour.

Thíra (Santoríni) Crater Cruise

This cruise gives superb views of the fantastically coloured volcanic cliffs of Thíra (Santoríni), with the white villages of Thíra and Oía clinging to the rim of the giant sea-filled crater – the most striking island landscape in the Aegean. Tickets for the trip are sold by tour agencies in Thíra and Kamári and at the larger resort hotels (if you are on a package tour they can be booked through your tour representative).

Boats depart from Skála Thíras, the small port at the foot of Santoríni's west coast cliffs, directly below Thíra. Most departures are at 9 or 9.30am, returning in the mid-afternoon.

1 DONKEY RIDE
A cobbled, zig-zag staircase descends for 270m from just below Thíra to the small pier at Skála Thíras. You will have to haggle

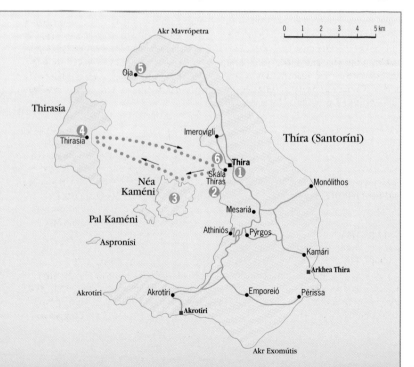

furiously over the price if the donkey ride is not included in the price of your excursion. Or, of course, you could simply walk down.

2 CRATER WALL
Leaving Skála Thíras, look back for a magnificent view of

The walls of Thíra's vast crater are banded with colours

the multicoloured, 270m high cliffs, banded with shades of red, pink, white, green and grey volcanic rock. Fragments of porous pumice stone can be seen floating in the bay.
After 15 to 20 minutes, land at Néa Kaméni, 2km west of Athiniós.

3 NÉA KAMÉNI
The eerie, lifeless island of shattered black rock is the product of a series of volcanic eruptions (see pages 68–9). Hot springs and boiling mud trickle from cracks in the rock and a smell of sulphur hangs over the islet. Just south and west of Néa Kaméni is the smaller Palaia Kaméni, also formed by vulcanism in the 2nd century BC.
The boat sails round Néa Kaméni's north coast heading west towards Thirasía. Look south for a view of Santoríni's dramatic southern cape, Akrotíri, where archaeologists have unearthed remains of a Minoan settlement almost 3,500 years old (see pages 66–7).

4 THIRASÍA
Thirasía is a tinier reflection of Santoríni. Its cliffs are all that remain of the original island, shattered by a titanic explosion 3,500 years ago. Like Thíra, the main village – also called Chóra – is reached by steep steps from the harbour below.

Pause here to get your breath back and enjoy the view across the crater. Chóra has several small, scenically located tavernas which will allow you to do just that while enjoying a cold drink.
Walk west and downhill across the island (30 to 45 minutes each way) to a choice of small pebbly and sandy coves on its western coast where you can swim and sunbathe, or take the less energetic option and swim from the tiny pier below Chóra, where the deep blue water is extremely clear and shoals of colourful fish make for excellent snorkelling.

5 OÍA
On the return boat trip, look north to the clifftop village of Oía perched on the extreme tip of Santoríni. It was shaken badly by tremors in 1956 but is now restored to pristine whiteness. Below the village at sea level, you can see the mouths of tunnels carved into the soft volcanic rock, used by the islanders as homes, stables and boathouses.

6 CABLE-CAR ASCENT
From Skála Thíras, take the dizzying cable-car ride from sea level to the cable-car station just below Thíra for a final view of Thirasía and the crater islands.

Kríti (Crete)

Crete is Greece's biggest island – more than 200km long from its western to its eastern tip. It's really a country within a country, with its own history, folklore and traditions. Only a very concise description of this most magnetic of islands is possible within this book: for a comprehensive guide to the island see the *Thomas Cook Travellers' Guide to Crete.*

Most of the hundreds of thousands who come to Crete each summer stay in the large resorts on the north coast. Holiday resorts have sprung up on south coast beaches too, but this part of the island is in general less developed: resorts and hotels are smaller and, except in high season, beaches are less crowded.

Inland, Crete is one of the most rewarding islands to explore, with soaring mountain ranges, remote hill-villages and hidden oasis-like valleys, lush with orange and lemon groves.

Its major towns are rewarding too, but in a different way. Crete was one of the jewels of Venice's Aegean empire, and from their mighty fortresses at Irakleío, Réthymno and Chaniá the Venetians held the island they called Candia until finally driven out by the Turks in 1669. Cretans rebelled repeatedly against the Turkish yoke and finally achieved *enosis* (union) with Greece in 1913.

From the late third millenium BC Crete was the seat of the Minoan empire – Europe's first civilisation – which

CRETE

The snow-capped White Mountains overlook Chaniá

controlled much of the Aegean from elaborate palaces such as Knosós and Faistós. After the collapse of the Minoan world around 1500BC (see pages 68–9) the island's importance faded until Roman times. As Rome's power dimmed it was ravaged by barbarian pirates, then in 823–4 seized by Arab invaders from Andalusia. The great Byzantine commander Nikiforos Fokas

recovered Crete in 961, then in 1204 it was seized from the crumbling Byzantine Empire by the Venetian Republic.

Crete is long and thin, lying east to west, and is the southernmost of the main Greek islands. In summer, it can be extremely hot. Spring comes early, in a blaze of wildflowers, and summer lasts longer than on any other island. As well as its treasury of ancient and medieval history, Crete has breathtaking mountain scenery amd wonderful beaches. On the north coast, Mália and Chersónisos are large-scale holiday resorts with long sandy beaches. Ágios Geórgios (Georgioupolis), also on the north coast, has a long stretch of fine sand too, but is not quite so built-up. On the south coast, the best sandy beach is at Mátala, with shingle and pebble beaches at Plakiás, Agía Galíni, and along the southwest coast.

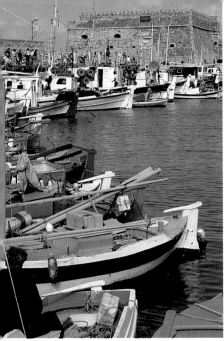

The 16th-century Venetian fortress guards the harbour at Irakleío

CHANIÁ (KHANIA)
Pretty, old-fashioned town with pastel-coloured neo-classical mansions around a harbour overlooked by Venetian walls. Immediately behind the harbour esplanade is an old quarter of narrow alleys and overhanging balconies weighted down with pots of flowers and herbs.
127km west of Irakleío.

Arkheologiko Moussío (Archaeological Museum)
Mysterious Minoan relics, Hellenistic marbles and Roman pottery and jewellery are on display here.
Halidhon, signposted, 100m from the harbour (tel: 0821 20334). Open: Tuesday to Friday 8.30am–3pm. Admission charge.

FAISTÓS (PHAESTOS)
Hilltop remains of a Minoan palace dating c2200–1700BC.

56km southwest of Irakleío (tel: 0892 22615). Open: weekdays 8am–5pm, weekends and holidays 8.30am–3pm. Admission charge.

GÓRTYS
Splendid ruins of a Hellenistic-Roman city with an early Christian basilica, temple foundations and agora.
44km south of Irakleío (tel: 081 226092). Open: daily 8.30am–3pm. Admission charge.

IRAKLEÍO (IRAKLION)
Crete's capital and main port is mainly commercial but a visit to its excellent museum and the colourful palace site at Knosós is essential.
Midway along the north coast.

Arkheologiko Moussío (Archaeological Museum)
Magnificent frescos from Knosós, mysterious Minoan seals and ornaments, statues and other finds from Hellenistic and Roman sites.
Just off Platía Eleftherias, signposted (tel: 081 226092). Open: Monday 11am–5pm, Tuesday to Friday 8am–5pm, weekends and holidays 8.30am–3pm. Admission free.

Arsenáli (Venetian Arsenal)
The great archways of the Venetian Arsenal (shipyard), now used for storing boats and fishing gear, overlook the old harbour.
Close to the foot of 25 Avgoustou. Freely accessible.

Koulos (Harbour Fortress)
The 16th-century castle is splendidly located, guarding the Venetian harbour. Its walls seem capable of resisting any bombardment.
At end of pier; access from junction of Venizelou and 25 Avgoustou (tel: 081 246211). Open: Tuesday to Sunday

8.30am–3pm. Admission charge.

Porta Khanion (Chaniá Gate)

Massive 17th-century Venetian ramparts ring the town centre and are easiest to see at Porta Khanion, where the main road passes through the old gateway Junction of 62 Martiron and Plastira. Bastions can also be seen at the eastern end of the walls at the junction of Makariou and Venizelou and at the western end at the junction of Venizelou and Doukous Bofor.

KNOSÓS

The most imaginatively reconstructed palace site in Greece, with colourful columns, halls and avenues of the millennia-old palace.

5km southeast of Irakleío. Bus 2 from city bus terminal, on Epimenidhou (tel: 081 231940). Open: daily 8am–7pm. Admission charge.

LASÍTHIOU

The verdant 'Plain of Windmills' , ringed by bare 1,000m-plus peaks, is still a joy, though most of the windmills are long gone and water is drawn to the fertile fields of this mountain oasis by petrol-driven pumps.

61km southeast of Irakleío.

Diktaío Spília (Dhikti Cave)

In this green, mossy 250m-deep cavern full of twisted stalagmites Zeus, king of the ancient gods, was born – or so legend has it. Less disputable are the relics that have been found indicating that people worshipped here from neolithic to Roman times.

1km above Psychró village car park, signposted. Steep path, mule hire available, torch recommended for cave (tel: 0834 31207). Open: daylight hours, July to September. Admission charge.

RÉTHYMNO (RETHIMNON)

The lanes and cobbled market streets of this old harbour town are overlooked by a mighty fortress and the older part of town, with its fountains, ramparts, palm trees and abandoned minarets, combines Turkish, Venetian and neo-classical influences.

95km west of Irakleío.

Arkheologiko Moussío (Archaeological Museum)

Coins from all eras are the centrepiece of a collection which also comprises sculpture, bronzes and jewellery.

Off Melissinou, opposite the southwest corner of the castle walls (tel: 0831-29975). Open: Tuesday to Sunday 8.30am–3pm. Admission charge.

Jami Nerandzi (Nerandzi Mosque)

Enjoy an overview of the harbour, old quarter and castle from the top of this slender Turkish survival.

West end of Mesolongiou. Minaret open: daily 11am–7pm. Admission free.

Kástro (Castle)

This is the largest Venetian castle ever built and dates from the late 16th century. Inside is a ghost town of barracks, churches and storerooms.

Open: daily, daylight hours. Admission free.

Detail on Irakleío's fortress

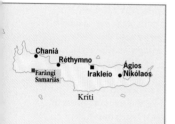

Farángi Samariás (Samaria Gorge)

This walk takes you through the most impressive mountain scenery in the Greek islands, from the top of the longest mountain gorge in Europe to the lovely pebble beach at Agía Rouméli. The gorge is a national park so camping, swimming in the freshwater pools and departing from the marked track are prohibited. Open: 1 May–mid-October depending on rainfall. *Allow 4 to 6 hours for this strenuous 18km walk.*

Start from Omalós village, 36km south of Chaniá. The head of the gorge is signposted Xylóskalo. On leaving the village you will receive a numbered ticket (no admission charge) which you surrender at the other end.

1 XYLÓSKALO (WOODEN STAIR)

The wooden steps, made of solid logs, start at 1,227m above sea level and drop steeply into the bottom of the gorge, turning into a footpath which descends almost 1,000m along a 2km stretch.

2 GÝNGILOS

Above you on your right, as you start the descent, is the towering flank of Mount Gýngilos, climbing to a sharp peak almost 1,000m above Omalós.
After the steep descent, the path becomes less tiring and zig-zags down grassy slopes, amid pine woods, with springs gurgling in the rocky streambed.

3 ÁGIOS NIKÓLAOS

The tiny whitewashed chapel of Ágios Nikólaos, with candles always burning in front of its icons, stands in a small pine wood to the right of the path.
After 1½ to 2 hours walking from Ágios Nikólaos, through rich-smelling pine forest and crossing the streambed, you will arrive at the deserted village of Samariá.

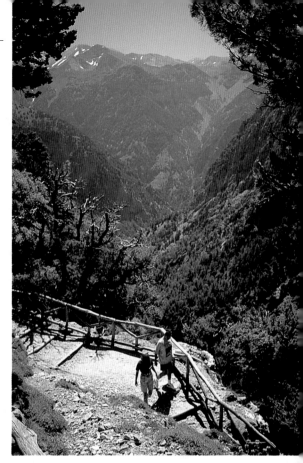

Xylóskalo, the wooden stair, drops steeply into the Samaria Gorge

4 SAMARIÁ

This ghost village, with its derelict stone cottages and abandoned mill and olive press, has been deserted for half a century. One house is used as the park warden's office. Samariá is the midway point of the walk, and there is an official picnic area under the pines where you can take a break.

From Samariá, the path passes another small chapel, Osia Marias, then winds along the streambed, crossing it several times by chains of water-smoothed boulders. The gorge narrows like a funnel, with the slopes either side becoming steeper until you reach the narrowest point.

5 SIDIRÓPORTES (IRON GATES)

The gorge is narrowest at this point. Grey cliff walls, marked with the rust-coloured stains of iron-bearing springs, shoot vertically to 600m. High above the sky is a narrow strip of blue. Water surging through the narrows makes the gorge impassable in winter and early spring, and even in summer you may have to take off your shoes and paddle across the stream.

From Sidiróportes the gorge fans out into a boulder-filled delta and the cliff walls recede to become steep rocky slopes, wooded in places. Walking is fairly easy for the final 5km to the sea at Agía Rouméli.

6 AGÍA ROUMÉLI

This tiny village exists only to service the steady flow of summer walkers. A chain of tavernas and small guesthouses extends the length of a pebbly beach ending in cliffs to the west but extending several kilometres eastward. The water is very clear and a swim is very welcome.

Independent travellers can opt to stay overnight at Agía Rouméli before walking on eastward to Chóra Sfákia, (where the road from Chaniá ends), or to travel on east or west by boat. Those on organised tours will be transferred by boat to Chóra Sfákia, to meet their coach.

Dodekánisos (Dodecanese)

*T*he Dodecanese island group contains something for everyone, with an array of landscapes ranging from the farmlands of Ródos (Rhodes) and Kós, to the stark hillsides of Kálymnos and the smouldering volcanic crater of Nísyros.

There are big, bright, beach resorts, miniature havens that see only one ferry a week, mosques and monasteries, ancient temples and medieval castles.

The chain of islands runs close to the Turkish coast in Greece's southeast Aegean, and the name 'Dodekánisos' means 'twelve islands' – but which 12? From south to north, the larger islands include Kásos, Kárpathos, Rhodes, Chálki, Tílos, Sými, Nísyros, Kós, Kálymnos, Léros and Pátmos. The twelfth, Astypálaia, far to the west, is technically part of the group but is closer to the Cyclades in character and is included in that section (see pages 54–5).

So far so good. But the Dodecanese also includes an assortment of tiny isles whose people are numbered only in hundreds or even in dozens. These include Megísti, Greece's easternmost outpost, within a few hundred metres of Turkey; Saría, off the north cape of Kárpathos; Psérimos, between Kálymnos and Kós; and the mini-archipelago of Leipsoí (Lipsi), Arkoí (Arki) and Agathónisi (Agathonisi), east of Pátmos.

Some of these, like Psérimos and Leipsoí, are close to popular vacation islands and are regularly invaded by flocks of day-trippers. Others, like Agathónisi or Arkoí, attract only the most determined of island-hopping solitude-seekers. Isolation and seclusion are their main attractions, and facilities

for tourists (where they exist at all) are usually modest (see pages 150–3). With frequent ferry and hydrofoil connections between the major islands and to Píreas and other island groups north and west, the Dodecanese group is perfect for island-hopping.

Man-made sights include the grand walled city of Rhodes, restored to its medieval splendour, the brooding fortified monastery of St John on Pátmos, and the ruins of classical, Hellenistic and Roman cities on Kós and Rhodes.

Dodecanese houses have a distinctive style of their own, typified by tall two- and three-storey homes with neo-classical stucco façades in pastel shades, high doors and shuttered windows. Many have wooden or wrought-iron balconies poised precariously above the street, and most have gardens or courtyards overflowing with vines, geraniums and often banana and palm trees. You will also see elaborate art-deco public buildings, built during the Italian occupation (1912–43).

The climate is mellower than that of the windswept islands of the central Aegean. The Dodecanese are spared the gusty *meltemi* which sometimes plagues the Cyclades, and Rhodes claims more hours of sunshine per year than anywhere else in Europe making it the only truly year-round holiday destination in the Greek islands.

DODECANESE

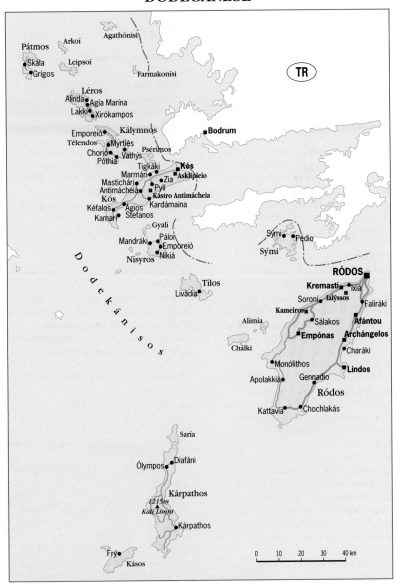

KÁLYMNOS

Kálymnos is an island of deep blue, fiord-like bays and striking bare white limestone hills, pock-marked with caves and dotted with green valley deltas of cultivation where the mountains meet the sea.

With so little fertile land, islanders have (until the advent of tourism) been dependent on the sea, and Kálymnos's sponge-divers ventured as far as the North African coast, Florida and even Cuba. These days the sponges which are sold everywhere on the island, are more likely to have been imported (many ironically from Florida) than to have been hauled up by local divers.
15km north of Kós.

CHORIÓ

Chorió is Kálymnos's medieval capital, built inland for protection from pirate raids. It is now a residential hillside suburb of Póthia, with many dignified old homes in tree-filled gardens.
3km northwest of Póthia.

Kástro

The small, crumbling castle is Byzantine, more than 1,000 years old, with Venetian additions dating from the 13th century. The heraldic arms of the Knights of St John are carved above the gateway.
200m above the village.
Freely accessible.

EMPOREIÓ

From its pebbly beach this tiny fishing hamlet (just waking up to the

possibilities of tourism) seems to be entirely land-locked, with steep hillsides rising to surround a deep, calm, crystal-clear inlet which offers fine swimming and snorkelling.
16km northwest of Póthia.

MASOURION AND MYRTIÉS (MIRTIES)

These two fishing hamlets lie at either end of a stretch of beach on a bay which is sheltered by the long, thin islet of Télendos. They have grown together into a pleasant small resort strip of small hotels, pensions and restaurants. The beaches are a mixture of pebbles and sand and the water is calm and very clear.
8 to 9km northwest of Póthia.

PÓTHIA

Prosperous from the 19th-century sponge trade, Póthia is a charmingly cluttered harbour surrounded by dolls' house-like mansions and cafés patronised by elderly traders and captains in panama hats or seamen's caps, many of them retired from sponge-fishing in Florida or the Bahamas.
On the south coast.

Dhimotikon (Town Hall)

The Town Hall is a fine example of the

Detail on the Castle of the Knights of St John

Barren hills rise behind Póthia, the sleepy harbour capital of Kálymnos

'art deco Moorish' style invented by the Italians for their public buildings in the Dodecanese, with elaborate domes, arches, round windows and plaster mouldings.
Midway along the harbour front.

Moussío Vouvalis (Vouvalis Museum)

An imposing and lavishly furnished mansion, once the home of Nikolaos Vouvalis, father of the island's sponge industry. He had offices in London and a business empire which stretched from Kálymnos, across the Saronic islands, as far as North Africa, Cuba, Nassau and Tarpon Springs, Florida. Portraits, paintings, documents and elaborate décor.
Signposted. Open: Monday to Friday 8.30am–3pm, weekends 8.30am–1pm. Admission charge.

Palaiókastro (Knights' Castle)

A crest of the Knights can be seen above the castle gateway. The ruined walls enclose a small Orthodox Chapel of the Panagía (Virgin).
2km northwest of Póthia. Freely accessible.

RINA

Rina is the miniature port of the farming settlement of Vathys. It's an enchanting ex-pirates' lair, where a narrow arm of the sea, only barely wide enough to allow fishing boats or yachts to pass, widens into an inner lagoon where boats bob. The cliffs shelter the inlet and the village and radiate the sun's heat in summer, even after sundown. Swim from the steps at the end of the pier, which lead into deep, clean water.
6km northeast of Póthia.

TÉLENDOS

Télendos, Kálymnos' tiny and mountainous satellite, shelters the waters off Myrtiés and Massouri and has beaches and a little hamlet of its own. There are regular small boats through the day in summer from Myrtiés.
1km west of Myrtiés.

KÁRPATHOS

Kárpathos is a lonely island. Long sea crossings separate it from its nearest large neighbours, Crete in the southwest and Rhodes in the northeast. Rugged and mountainous, it has excellent beaches and attractive villages. A charter airport ensures that despite its remoteness by sea it gets its share of tourism, but as Kárpathos is the second largest of the Dodecanese (after Rhodes), it absorbs its summer visitors without becoming overcrowded.

An island of changing landscapes, its fertile southern half is connected to the more barren and mountainous north by a knife-edged mountain ridge which in places is just wide enough to carry the road. Bus rides can be vertigo-inducing. In the north is one of the island's highest peak, Profítis Ilías, reaching 1,140m.

Like many islands, Kárpathos lost many of its people to emigration in the 19th and early 20th century, most of them heading for the eastern United States, which is why you may meet older men, retired to their island birthplace, speaking fluent English with Brooklyn and New Jersey accents. Many family homes have been colourfully rebuilt with money earned overseas. Local tastes run to vivid blue and green plasterwork, domes and archways, offset by purple and crimson bougainvillaea.

Though Kárpathos shares some of the history of its Dodecanese neighbours to the east, with occupation by Byzantines, Venetians, Knights of St John and Turks, none of them left much in the way of tangible remains. Kárpathos makes up for that by offering walkers the finest rambles in the Dodecanese, whether in the gentler valleys and vineyards of the south or in the breathtaking

mountainscapes of the north.
60km southwest of Rhodes.

AMOPI

Kárpathos's growing holiday resort has a choice of three sandy beaches and an increasing number of hotels and tourist tavernas.
8km south of Pigádia (Kárpathos Town).

ÓLYMPOS

The principal village in northern Kárpathos, Ólympos is awesomely situated on a high, windy ridge which plunges sheer to the west coast of the island. A line of stone windmills stands along the ridge, some of them still in use. Above the village is the peak of Profítis Ilías, the island's highest point. Ólympos was one of the most isolated villages in the Aegean until the building of the road from Pigádia in 1980. Its small port, Diafáni, 3km away on the east coast, is too small for inter-island ferries to dock. As a result, it retains much of the old-fashioned self-sufficiency and many of its traditions, including village women in local costumes (see page 144).
40km north of Pigádia.

PIGÁDIA (KÁRPATHOS TOWN)

The capital is a well-kept, unassuming modern harbour where boats call en route between Rhodes and Crete. Its redeeming feature is its proximity to the

A line of dilapidated windmills stands on the ridge above Ólympos on Kárpathos

fine, 2km sandy beach of Órmos Vrondis, which begins immediately north of the harbour.
On the southwest coast.

VROUKOUNDA (VRYCHONTA)
These scattered ruins of various eras include the foundations of a small temple, a Byzantine-Turkish keep, rock graves and a shrine to Áyios Ioannis Theológos (St John the Divine) in a cliff cave.
North of Pigádia. Freely accessible.

KÁSOS

This southernmost island of the Dodecanese group is a delight for island purists. Here tourism has had zero impact. There are no sights to see and nothing to do except ramble among tiny fields and olive groves, sit in cafés and tavernas, and swim and sunbathe.
10km south of Kárpathos.

FRÝ
The island capital is ringed by mountains and set on a rocky bay, enlivened only by infrequent ferries from Crete and Kárpathos. Its dignified older homes belong to ship-owning families whose fleets brought some prosperity to the island in the 19th century and its port, Emporeió, is a 10-minute walk away.

KÓS

Kós, the third largest of the Dodecanese, is a long, fish-shaped island of changing landscapes. The higher slopes of Mount Dikios (Óros Díkeos), which dominates the northeast of the island, are rugged and treeless, while its lower slopes are covered by pine and fig-trees. Northwestern Kós is covered by wheat fields and cattle pasture. Inland, much of the island is a high, breezy plateau of meadows, thorn-trees and goat pasture. The southern tip is mountainous, but its shores are studded with small beaches.

There are excellent beaches all over Kós, and the island is a favourite holiday destination for northern Europeans.

Like Rhodes, Kós was a stronghold of the Knights of St John, who left behind two formidable castles. Turkish and Italian occupiers also left their mark.

In 1933 the island was struck by an earthquake which levelled much of Kós Town, thus allowing the Italian authorities to open up sites for archaeological excavation which might otherwise be still uninvestigated. Part of the island capital's charm is due to the casual array of ruins next to everyday streets.

Midway up the chain of the Dodecanese, Kós has excellent connections by ferry and hydrofoil

Shepherds on muleback guard their flocks on Kós's rugged hills

to its neighbours and westwards to the Cyclades and Athens, making it a popular island-hopping junction.

Kálymnos, Psérimos and Nísyros are all close enough to be popular day-trip destinations, as is Bodrum in Turkey. *110km northwest of Rhodes.*

KARDÁMAINA

Kós's biggest and busiest resort features long, southeast-facing beaches to either side of a small fishing harbour, surrounded by a long strip of bars, discos, hotels and restaurants. The resort has grown too fast to have kept much of its local character. Until the late 1970s it was no more than a village. Today it could be anywhere in Greece. The conical silhouette of the isle of Nísyros (see pages 96–7) can be seen on the southern horizon and excursion boats depart daily to here from Kardámaina harbour in summer.
25km southwest of Kós Town.

KÁSTRO ANTIMÁCHEIA (ANDIMACHIA CASTLE)

The impressive angular battlements surrounding the hilltop date from the mid-14th century. The Knights of St John rebuilt the castle in the 15th century and the crest of Grand Master del Caretto is carved above the main gate, (which itself is within a much later Italian gun-casement). The small chapel of Agía Paraskevi within the

Beach umbrellas line Paradise Beach, one of the prettiest on Kós

ramparts, dates from 1494.
18km southwest of Kós Town, 4km northeast of Kardámaina. Freely accessible.

KÉFALOS

Kéfalos is a relaxed small resort overlooking one of the island's best beaches, the long south-facing strip of Kamari. It is the best place on Kós for a quieter holiday, avoiding the crowds and the frenzied nightlife of Kardámaina. There are other beaches to the north and south, reached on foot over hill paths, or by small boats which operate frequently throughout the summer.
45km southwest of Kós Town.

Ágios Stefanos (Basilica of St Stephen)

Ruins comprising the walls and columns of a 5th-century Christian basilica.
North end of Kamári Bay, next to the Club Mediterranée resort. Freely accessible.

Palatia (Ancient Kós)

A 4th-century BC sanctuary of Demeter and the tiered seats of an ancient theatre have been excavated at the site of the island's first city. In 366BC the capital of the island was moved to the site of modern Kós Town.
2km southeast of Kéfalos. Freely accessible.

KÓS TOWN (CHÓRA)

The modern capital is an agreeable blend of Greek and Roman ruins, medieval fortifications, Turkish leftovers and florid Italian public buildings. Mingle in with the everyday bustle around the crescent harbour and the busy market area where high-piled produce stalls, gaudy souvenir stores and smart goldsmiths' shops stand next to each other.
East end of the island.

Agorá

The site of the Hellenistic agorá (marketplace), dating from the 4th century BC, contains foundations of several temples, sections of the town walls, a Christian basilica and the extensive foundations of the Roman city of Kós.
Access from Platía Eleftherias, signposted (tel: 0242 28763). Open: Tuesday to Sunday 8.30am–3pm. Admission charge.

**Arkheologiko Moussío
(Archaeological Museum)**

The main exhibits are the 4th-century BC statue of Hippokrates and a mosaic of Asklipios (see Asklipieío). Other finds span the 3rd century BC to the 2nd century AD.

Platia Eleftherias (tel: 0242 28326). Open: Tuesday to Sunday 8.30am–3pm. Admission charge.

Asklipieío

This is one of the best preserved and most beautifully located sacred places in the Aegean islands. Seven white Corinthian columns of a 2nd-century AD Roman temple have been re-erected and the arched walls of the ancient terrace have been rebuilt. Two columns of the 4th-century BC Temple of Asklipios (god of healing), can also be seen.

4km southwest of town centre, signposted (tel: 0242 28763). Open: Tuesday to Sunday 8.30am–3pm. Admission charge.

Casa Romana

A reconstruction of a 3rd-century AD Roman villa with mosaics, three inner courtyards and baths.

Grigorioutou Pemptou (tel: 0242 28326). Open: Tuesday to Sunday 8.30am–3pm. Admission charge.

Kástro

The medieval Knights' castle, a low square of sloping ramparts and turreted bastions, guards the harbour.

South side of harbour (tel: 0242 28326). Open: Tuesday to Sunday 8.30am–3pm. Admission charge.

Odeion

The odeion (Roman theatre) has 14 tiers of marble seats. Opposite, on the other side of Grigorioutou Pemptou, is a second extensive archaeological site, covered with a confusing clutter of marble capitals and fallen columns.

West end of Grigorioutou Pemptou (tel: 0242 28763). Open: Tuesday to Sunday 8.30am–3pm. Admission charge.

Palm trees and bougainvillaea brighten the Castle of the Knights

Fast hydrofoils link Kós with its Dodecanese neighbours to north and south

MARMÁRI

Kós's west coast is an almost continuous strip of sandy beaches, but prevailing strong winds make them less popular among holidaymakers than the more sheltered strands of the southeast. There are exceptions, and Marmári is one of them. Windsurfers rate it among the best in Europe for its steady breezes.
Southwest coast, 15km southwest of Kós Town.

MASTICHÁRI

An unassuming port with a small beach, Mastichári's main attraction is the ferries which leave regularly for Kálymnos and the little island of Psérimos. Southwest of Mastichári the coast is windswept and unappealing.
West coast, 30km southwest of Kós Town.

PYLÍ

The ruined ghost village of old Pylí on the southwest shoulder of Óros Díkeos (Mount Dikios) is appealing in a tumbledown way. Hidden in a wooded glen, it is surmounted by the shell of a Byzantine tower. Half a dozen small chapels indicate that the village was quite prosperous in its medieval heyday, when its inhabitants huddled below the protecting castle to escape marauders from the sea. Unfortunately their wall-paintings are not well preserved.
1km southeast of modern Pylí, 23km southwest of Kós Town.

TIGKÁKI

The best beach close to Kós Town. Tigkáki is sandy, but like all the west coast beaches can be blustery too.
12km west of Kós Town.

ZIA

Zia is the most visited and the prettiest of the villages of Mount Dikeos. By night tour coaches arrive for 'typical Greek evenings' in recently-built tavernas. Come here in the daytime, for the fine mountain scenery and the views of the island and of its northern neighbours.
12km southwest of Kós Town.

LÉROS

Léros is a peaceful island which sees far fewer visitors than its neighbours to the north and south. Its beaches, if not breathtaking, are certainly uncrowded, and its harbour towns, if not over-endowed with purpose-built tourism attractions and facilities, are undeniable slices of authentic Greek island life.

There's also a fertile hinterland of rolling hills, terraced fields and olive groves, which is ideal if you like undemanding rambles in a rural setting. This is one island where the locals still outnumber the visitors all year round.

Léros's coastline is deeply indented, making it look like a piece from a jigsaw puzzle, and though it is only 17km from its northern to southern tip it has more than 70km of coastline. The superb anchorage at Lakkí, on the west coast, made the island a strategic prize in World War II. The events on which the book and film *The Guns of Navarone* are loosely based, took place here when in 1943, following the Italian capitulation, British troops attempted to occupy the island before it could be secured by Germany, only to be expelled by a stronger and better-supported German force. The islanders and their homes suffered severely in the fierce fighting.

AGÍA MARÍNA (PLATANOS)

Agía Marína, Léros's eastern port, is really three villages which have merged into one higgledy-piggledy town spanning a hilly, castle-topped headland with harbours on either side. Agía Marína surrounds the main northern harbour; Pandeli lies on a smaller fishing harbour; Platanos, below the castle on the headland, separates Pandeli and Agía Marína.
East coast.

Kástro (Platanos Castle)

The first castle on this site was built by the Byzantines, but the tower and ramparts which now crown the village were strengthened by the Venetians and the Knights of St John, and is again being restored. It is still garrisoned by the Greek Army, as its location, with panoramic views over many kilometres, makes it a perfect lookout point.

Within the castle is a small museum exhibiting pottery and other finds from excavations around the island and a small monastery church, Panayía (Church of the Virgin). No monks live here any more but there is a reputedly miraculous icon of the Virgin. (Church open irregular hours.)
Immediately above centre of Platanos, signposted from Platanos. Open:

An unusual combination of two familiar images

Bright yellow nets at Agía Marína, Léros's main harbour

dawn to dusk. Admission free. Note: photography forbidden.

ALINDA
The best beach on the island and its only developed resort, Alinda has a narrow, shingly beach and attractive views across the bay to the castle at Agía Marína (Platanos), Léros's only historic sight.
4km northwest of Agía Marína.

LAKKÍ
Lakkí, on one of the finest natural harbours in the Eastern Mediterranean, is a near ghost town with the languid atmosphere of a deserted film set. Grandiose public buildings and an open-air cinema behind a crumbling art-deco façade (the style chosen by the Italians for their Aegean possessions) are dotted about a grid of wide, dusty boulevards, lined with palm and eucalyptus trees. It has an unfinished look, perhaps not surprisingly, as Italy's Aegean adventure, which began with the seizure of the Dodecanese from Turkey in 1912, ended ignominiously in 1943.
West coast, 4km south of Agía Marína.

XIRÓKAMPOS
The coast of the neighbouring isle of Kálymnos, not far south, appears to almost lock in the narrow bay of Xirókampos, where an unassuming farming village sits among fields and palm trees behind a long, narrow beach.
10km south of Agía Marína.

The brilliant white village of Emporeió perches above the volcano

NÍSYROS

The tiny southern neighbour of Kós, Nísyros is blessed with a charm out of all proportion to its size.

Its conical slopes surround a vast inner hollow, in the very centre of which a crater of sulphurous mud bubbles alarmingly. By contrast picturesque white villages cling to the rim of the crater, looking outward over thickly wooded slopes.

The island's volcanic soil is extremely fertile, and this, together with earnings from the cement quarries on the islet of Gyalí has given Nísyros, a degree of peaceful prosperity.

Seen from a distance, the thick bush clinging to its slopes makes the island look almost tropical, though its beaches don't live up to this first impression, comprising pebbles and brownish sand. As a result, Nísyros sees few tourists apart from excursionists from Kós, who make a flying visit to the crater before heading back, and it still feels pleasantly remote from 'civilisation'.
12km south of Kós.

EMPOREIÓ

This almost deserted village has one small café among tumbledown houses and spectacular views out to sea and the Kós coast. For equally awesome views down into the old crater with its patchwork of fields, follow the whitewashed steps to the highest point of the village, where there is a pretty hilltop church in good repair.
6km east of Mandráki.

KRATEIR (CRATER)

Around the crater the hillsides are streaked with sulphur and the air smells like the aftermath of a fireworks display. The crater itself is a bowl 250m wide and 30m deep. Fumaroles emit steam from deep underground and grey mud, stained by brimstone-yellow sulphur deposits, heaves and bubbles. Here at the bottom, the ground temperature can reach 120°C.

Near by, an EU-funded project aims to harness the crater's geothermal energy.
Centre of the island. Freely accessible.

MANDRÁKI

Most of the island's 900 or so inhabitants live here in the main village, a network of narrow lanes and squares rising uphill from the esplanade, where fish tavernas sit by the sea-wall. These look north to Kós and the strange silhouette of the quarry island Gyalí. The harbour, where ferries and excursion boats from Kós dock, is about 750km east of the village.
Northwest corner of the island.

Historiko kai Laografiko Moussío (Historical and Ethnographical Museum)

A restored village home with traditional interiors and furnishings.
Signposted between village centre and Panagía Spiliani. Open: irregular hours. Admission charge.

Palaiókastro

Grim ramparts of spectacular black volcanic rock guard the island's oldest defensive site. It has been fortified throughout the ages, from the Dorian era (2,600 years ago), to the days of the Venetians and the Knights of St John.
1km south of the village, signposted. Freely accessible.

Panagia Spiliani (Church of the Virgin of the Cave)

Built into the mountain, within battlements erected by the Knights of St John, this monastery church dates from 1600 and has a valuable iconostasis.
Overlooking the village (signposted). Open: daily, daylight hours. Admission charge.

NIKIÁ

This spectacularly located village makes a dazzling splash of white against the rugged mountainscape of the crater rim.
10km southeast of Mandráki.

Moní Ágios Ioannis Theológos (Monastery of St John)

A whitewashed monastery church, perched precariously on the upper slopes, looking down into the crater.
500m below Nikiá, on the signposted path to the crater. Not usually open.

PÁLOI

This little fishing village has a large harbour where traditional wooden fishing boats are built and yachts anchor, plus an esplanade lined with tamarisk trees and, to the east, its long brownish sandy beach is the most easily accessible on Nísyros.
3km east of Mandráki.

Blue-painted balconies in Mandráki's main street

PÁTMOS

Pátmos is an island of great natural and man-made beauty, crowned by the ramparts of an impressive medieval monastery and by the most striking village in the Dodecanese.

On the coast, lovely blue bays almost cut Pátmos in two and there are lots of secluded little beaches. Inland low rocky hills are covered with terraced fields, divided by a maze of dry-stone walls topped with thorns. Ranks of eucalyptus trees, a late introduction, shade island streets and fig trees, bougainvillaea and prickly pear cluster around houses and villages.

The fact that Pátmos has been proclaimed a holy island, maintains monastic conservatism and has no airport have all kept tourism quite low-key, however the legendary monastery does make it one of the better known islands in the Dodecanese chain.
60km northwest of Kós.

GRÍGOS
Pátmos's best and most accessible beach is within a steep-sided east coast bay. The setting is hard to beat, though the beach is pebbly and no better than average.
5km south of Skála.

PÁTMOS TOWN (CHÓRA)
The hilltop village of Pátmos Town is one of the most beautiful in Greece, well worth the steep walk up from Skála. Tall mansions in grey stone and white plaster date from its 17th-century heyday, when islanders owned a substantial merchant fleet. Around them are simpler village homes. The colours are austere, an almost monochrome mix of white walls and grey stone doorways and arches, and it is almost impossible to keep a sense of direction in these corridor-like lanes, stairs and passages. Pátmos Town – like many old Greek villages – is much bigger than it appears at first sight. To find your way out of the maze, just keep heading downhill.
1 to 2km above Skála.

Moní Ágios Ioannis Theológos (Monastery of St John the Divine)

The grand monastery around which Chóra is built is Pátmos's claim to fame. Founded in the 11th century, it was self-governing under the Byzantine emperors and kept its independence when the Venetian Dukes of Náxos acquired Pátmos in the 13th

Gorgeous mosaics decorate the Monastery of St John

Deep blue bays make Skála a perfect anchorage, almost cutting Pátmos in two

century. Its grim black battlements and bastions make it look more like a fortress than a place of worship. They were built to protect the treasures of the monastery from pirate raids and were added to throughout the Middle Ages, with the great sloping buttresses dating from the 16th century.

Inside the walls is a central courtyard lined with domed arcades and paved with a mosaic of black pebbles. The Katholikon (main church) of the monastery stands to the left of this courtyard. Built in 1090, its interior is decorated with 17th-century frescos of the life of St John. The chapel of the Virgin, part of the main church, has remarkable late 12th-century frescos, revealed and restored in 1958.

Next to the Katholikon is the monastery museum, which has a gorgeous collection of icons, holy vestments, and church furniture. *Centre of the village (signposted). Open: daily 8am–noon, 3–6pm (afternoon hours may vary). Admission charge.*

SKÁLA

The island's main village and harbour is on a perfect anchorage which makes it a popular port of call for yachts. It's an attractive verdant, flower-filled village and its handful of medium-sized hotels are unobtrusive among the more traditional whitewashed buildings. The harbourside is lined with café tables which, after dark, attract a more stylish clientele than you would expect on this remote little island, many of them Athenians and foreigners who own homes in Pátmos Town (see opposite).

The grand black battlements of the Monastery of St John frown down on Skála from its hilltop site.
East coast.

THE KNIGHTS OF ST JOHN

Founded to succour wounded Crusaders and pilgrims in the Holy Land, the Knights of St John were expelled from Palestine after the fall of Acre in 1291 and settled on Cyprus until they transferred to Rhodes in 1309. Seizing the Dodecanese as well as the port of Bodrum on the Turkish coast, they built new castles or strengthened existing fortifications on almost all the islands. They also built a city of palaces and lodges – one for each of the 'tongues' of the order – within the great ramparts of Rhodes.

Each tongue represented one of the eight different nationalities – Aragon, Auvergne, Castile, England, France, Germany, Italy and Provence – whose lodges and crests you can see on Odós Ippóton, the restored Street of the Knights in the old town of Rhodes.

There were never more than 650 Knights of the Order in total, though with their wealth they commanded a fighting force of much greater numbers.

The Knights ruled the seas of the Eastern Aegean for the next two centuries and though they claimed to be defenders of Christendom their galleys preyed on any vessels they could catch, including those of Greek islanders and

The Knights' strongholds:
Castle of the Knights of St
John at Líndos (far left);
Rhodes Old Town (bottom);
detail in the Street of the
Knights in Rhodes.
Left: Knights taking Rhodes
from the Turks

merchants. In 1522,
however, Suleiman the
Magnificent attacked
Rhodes with a huge fleet
and a 100,000-strong
army. Only 200 Knights
survived the six-month
siege, finally withdrawing
after a negotiated
surrender. Vastly
outnumbered, it was a tribute to their
fighting prowess and to the strength
of their defences that they held out
so long. The huge stone
cannonballs fired by the Turkish
siege guns can still be seen littering the
dry moat around the old quarter.

The Knights later moved to Malta,
granted to them in 1530 by the Holy
Roman Emperor Charles V. Though
their piratical ways did not endear them
to their Greek neighbours, Mussolini
decided that they were suitable militant
role models for Fascist Italy and under
the Italian occupation of Rhodes the
battlemented Palace of the Grand
Masters, the lodges of the eight
'tongues' and other relics of the Knights
were painstakingly restored, which
explains why they are in such good
repair compared with most other
medieval buildings in the Greek islands.

Ródos (Rhodes)

*T*he biggest and most important of the Dodecanese chain, Rhodes has some of Greece's best beaches, a fascinating intact medieval city, more sunshine than any other island, and, in Líndos, the most picturesque of island village resorts.

The eponymous capital of the island is really two towns rolled into one. The restored medieval quarter, within the 14th-century ring of walls built by the Knights of St John, is an eye-catching mix of historic buildings, museums, colourful shopping streets and unchanged old-fashioned homes and workshops in narrow alleys. Plentiful palm trees plus mosques and minarets (a few still used by the city's handful of Muslims), give the old quarter a distinctly eastern flavour.

In classical times the island was divided between three powerful city states – Ialýssos, Líndos and Kameíros – which banded together in 408BC to build a new capital, Rhodes, on the site of today's city. Remnants of the ancient capital can be seen on the slopes of Monte Smith and at a newly discovered site on Odós Panetiou.

The new town, built around the Mandráki harbour, is a more commonplace blend of homes, shops, hotels, restaurants, bars and discos behind a rather grand waterfront of pompous Italianate public buildings and arcaded cafés.

Large holiday resorts spread either side of Rhodes Town on both the east and west

Bronze deer, the emblem of Rhodes, stand guard over Mandráki harbour

RHODES

coasts of the island, and Líndos is the hub of a second concentration of resort beaches. The west coast, often windswept where it is not mountainous, is less-visited, and inland, especially the south, is a different world of rolling hills and farms.

Rhodes's smaller satellites, Sými, Chálki and Tílos, are within easy reach by hydrofoil, fast catamaran or ferry and a small fleet of excursion vessels sets out daily from Mandráki harbour each morning.

AFÁNTOU

Popular Afántou with its long shingle beach is less crowded than other beaches nearer Rhodes Town and is somewhat less built-up. Small pebbly coves at either end of the bay offer potential privacy.
22km south of Rhodes Town.

CHARÁKI

An unexploited fishing hamlet, Charáki has an excellent empty sweep of clean, pebbly beach beside its little harbour. The shell of a small castle of the Knights, standing on a low hill at its north end, adds a little historic colour.
East coast, 40km south of Rhodes Town.

FALIRÁKI

The island's biggest and noisiest resort appeals to an international clientele in search of watersports, beach-life and a vivacious after-dark scene. The beach, long and of coarse sand, with an excellent choice of watersports, is the main attraction and is crowded for almost the whole season.
East coast, 12km south of Rhodes Town.

IALÝSSOS (ANCIENT IALYSOS)

Foundations of a 3rd-century BC Temple of Athene and Zeus and a fine Doric well-house from 300BC are highlights of this site.
15km southwest of Rhodes Town (tel:0241 21954). Open: Tuesday to Sunday 8.30am–3pm. Admission charge.

IXIÁ

The first resort outside Rhodes Town on the west coast is a virtual suburb of the city and has most of the island's international luxury-class hotels, with amenities such as landscaped grounds and swimming pools – just as well, since the beach here is long but narrow and gritty.
West coast, 3 to 4km south of Rhodes Town.

KAMEÍROS

The graceful columns and foundations of the ancient city of Kameíros have been excavated and partly restored by Italian archaeologists, and stand within later medieval walls.
35km southwest of Rhodes Town, signposted from main coast road (tel: 0241 21954). Open: Tuesday to Sunday 8.30am–3pm. Admission charge.

LÍNDOS

The prettiest village on Rhodes and one of the most charming in Greece, Líndos is noted for its unique homes, built around courtyards with elaborate mosaics in black and white pebbles. Traffic is banned in the village centre, and the

The ancient acropolis and 15th-century fortress above Líndos

Graceful 3rd-century BC columns mark the site of the Temple of Apollo

village is well-kept and clean though completely taken over by tourism.

Acropolis

The Acropolis of Líndos is built on a 180m-high sea cliff, protected by impregnable 15th-century battlements. The Gothic gate and stair and a partially ruined church of St John stand among the ruins of the 5th-century BC temple precinct ruins. High points are the 2nd-century BC 'Ship of Líndos', a relief of a galley carved into the rock by the main gate, and on the highest point the columns of the 4th-century BC Doric Temple of Athene.

Within the walls of the castle, immediately above the village, signposted (tel: 0241 21954). Open: Tuesday to Sunday 8.30am–3pm. Admission charge.

MONÓLITHOS CASTLE

This ghostly, abandoned 15th-century castle was built by the Knights on a pine-covered crag to watch over the southern

part of the west coast.

83km southwest of Rhodes Town (signposted). Freely accessible.

MONTE SMITH (ÁGIOS STEFANOS)

Three slender 3rd-century BC columns on the hillside mark the site of the Temple of Apollo and the ancient acropolis of Rhodes. Below them lie the restored 3rd-century BC stadium and odeon (theatre).

1km southwest of Rhodes Town (tel: 0241 21954). Open: 8.30am–3pm. Admission free.

PETALOÚDES (VALLEY OF THE BUTTERFLIES)

Despite the valley's popular name, the colourful scarlet-winged insects which swarm here in July and August are in fact tiger moths. Outside the moth season, when no coach parties visit the valley, it is a pleasant green retreat.

26km southwest of Rhodes Town. Open: 8am–sunset. Admission charge.

Rhodes Old Town

This walk takes in the high points of the picturesque old quarter, with a look at ancient relics, medieval fortifications, and Turkish survivals. High points include the various Inns (headquarters and lodgings) of the 'tongues' of the Knights, and the restored Palace of the Grand Masters. *Allow 2½ hours, plus half an hour for the Archaeological Museum and time for shopping on Odós Sokrátous.*

1 PÍLI NAVARHÍOU

Enter the Old Town by Píli Navarhíou (Admiral's Gate), off the south end of Mandráki harbour. An arched stone bridge crosses the dry moat, where a small herd of deer – once the sacred animal of the city – are kept.

Pass through the arched gateway which pierces the massive walls to enter Platía Alexándrou.

2 PAND AUVERGNE (INN OF THE AUVERGNE)

The arched doorway of the 14th-century inn leads off the small square into a courtyard with a fountain made of marble blocks taken from early Byzantine churches. The façade of the Inn of the Auvergne is on the east side of the square. On the west side is the arsenal (armoury) of the knights, an impressive 14th-century building which now contains the Museum of Decorative Arts.

3 ARMÉRIA (ARSENAL AND MUSEUM OF DECORATIVE ARTS)

The arms of Roger de Pinsot, Grand Master of the Knights of St John from 1355 to 1365, stand above the doorway. The museum contains fine examples of Rhodian pottery, furniture and traditional costumes.

Leaving Platía Alexándrou by the southwest corner, pause at the Archaeological Museum before turning right on to the long cobbled prospect of Odós Ippóton.

Rhodes Old Town is a living museum of medieval buildings

4 MOUSSÍO ARKHEOLOGIKÓ (ARCHAEOLOGICAL MUSEUM)

The Archaeological Museum is housed in the former Hospital of the Knights, a grand Gothic building dating from the late 15th century and displaying the arms of Jean de Lastic, Grand Master from 1437–54. The museum, housed on the lower floor, displays a fine assortment of statuary including the masterly Aphrodite of Rhodes, a 1st-century BC statue of the goddess.

5 ODÓS IPPOTÓN (STREET OF THE KNIGHTS)

The eight different orders all had their lodges (or inns) on this long street, leading uphill from the Hospital and Arsenal to the Palace of the Grand Masters. Turrets, gargoyles and carved coats of arms above each arched doorway mark the inns of each 'tongue'.

6 PALÁTI MEGÁLON MAGISTRON (PALACE OF THE GRAND MASTERS)

Square towers, crenellated walls and sturdy bastions protect the fortress-like palace. The first-floor state rooms contain marvellously restored Hellenistic and Roman mosaics.

Walk 250m south on Odós Panetiou. The dome of Tzamí Souleïmán (Mosque of Suleiman) is a landmark at its southern end.

7 TZAMÍ SOULEÏMÁN (MOSQUE OF SULEIMAN)

The building, converted into a mosque in 1522 following Suleiman's conquest of the city, is elegantly decorated in pale yellow and pink. Originally a Church of the Apostles, it has a fine Italian Renaissance gate.

Turn left on to Odós Sokrátous, the town's main shopping street, lined with jewellers, antique and souvenir shops, designer-clothes stalls and leatherwear boutiques. At the foot of Sokrátous, leave the old town by Píli Agías Ekaterínis.

MOSQUES AND MUSLIMS

Minarets and domes among the palm trees are a reminder of the island's Turkish past. Unlike mosques elsewhere in the islands, some of those on Rhodes are still used by worshippers. Rhodes has quite a large Muslim population, originally dating from the 16th-century conquest, and boosted in 1913 by Greek and Turkish Muslims driven from their homes on Crete in an early act of ethnic cleansing following its union with Greece. These settled in Rhodes and the Néa Kritika (New Cretan) district on the road to the airport is still a largely Muslim community.

The colourful Tzamí Souleïman (Mosque of Suleiman) is one of the Old Town's major landmarks, while the leaning turban-topped headstones of the overgrown Muslim cemetery (near the junction of Eleftherias and Vassileos Konstantinou, west of Mandráki harbour), is another relic.

The Mosque of Suleiman was built anew to mark the Turkish conquest of the island by Suleiman the Magnificent in 1522, but many other mosques in the Turkish quarter were

Greece's Muslim legacy can be seen on Rhodes, Kós and Crete: the Suleiman Mosque (above) and Turkish cemetery, Rhodes Old Town (left); Defterdar Mosque, Kós Town (far left); Mosque of Nerantzies, Rethimnon, Crete (right)

originally Orthodox churches, and fine Byzantine frescos have been discovered beneath plaster in the disused Pegial el Din and Ilk Mihrab mosques.

On Sokrátous, the shopping street in the heart of the Old Town, the Aga Mosque is still used by local devout Muslims, and other surviving mosques are dotted around the Old Town, which became a purely Muslim quarter after the Turkish conquest.

Platía Aronos, in the old quarter. Open: 7am–7pm. Admission charge; soap and towel extra.

Kós Old Town

One of the charms of the island capital is the clutter of medieval and ancient sites painstakingly uncovered after the 1933 earthquake. This easy walk takes in the highlights (see pages 91–3). *Allow 2 hours.*

Start from the south side of the harbour, beneath the castle, whose ramparts are the town's most obvious landmark.

1 KÁSTRO (CASTLE OF THE KNIGHTS OF ST JOHN)

Inner and outer ramparts were built between 1450 and 1478 using many blocks looted from ancient temples. Impregnable towers at each corner strengthen the mighty defences, and with this castle and its twin at Halikarnassos (modern Bodrum, Turkey) the knights controlled the strategic strait between Kós and the mainland.

Leave the castle by the wooden footbridge, crossing the dry moat to reach Platía tou Platanou, the small square leading to the first archaeological site.

2 PLATÍA TOU PLATANOU (HIPPOKRATES' TREE)

The giant plane tree, its great boughs spreading to shade the

entire square, clings stubbornly to life although its trunk is completely hollow and its branches are supported by scaffolding. To have shaded Hippokrates it would have to be more than 2,400 years old, making it perhaps the oldest tree in Europe.
Cross the square to enter the first of the Old Town's two archaeological sites.

3 AGORÁ ARCHAEOLOGICAL SITE

This was the site of the Roman town and was strikingly designed with a flight of broad steps connecting it with the harbour. The street plan, including foundations of temples and civic buildings and paving from ancient streets can be clearly seen. Near by, within the same site, are the foundations of the Hellenistic agorá (marketplace), including the toppled columns and column bases of several temples.
Leave the site by the Platía Eleftherias gate. The Archaeological Museum is on the north side of the square, signposted.

4 MOUSSÍO ARKHEOLOGIKÓ (ARCHAEOLOGICAL MUSEUM)

A rich and varied collection of Roman and Hellenistic sculpture depicts Hippokrates, Hygieia (Goddess of Health) and Hermes (messenger of the gods), while a colourful mosaic of Hippokrates and Asklipios (the god of healing), decorates the courtyard.

5 DEFTERDAR MOSQUE

The dome and minaret of the Defterdar mosque, built in the 18th century, stand above Platía Eleftherias on its south side. The arcaded ground floor of the once-grand mosque is occupied by small shops.
Leave Platía Eleftherias by the west side, turning on to the pedestrian Odós Ifestou.

Tumbled columns lie within the medieval Castle of the Knights

6 ODÓS IFESTOU (BAZAAR)

Originally the heart of the medieval Turkish bazaar area, the modern pedestrian street is mainly taken up by souvenir stores and jewellery boutiques. Reminders of the Turkish era include a fountain with Koranic inscription (where Ifestou meets Venizelou) and a lone minaret close to the west end of Ifestou.
At the west end of Ifestou cross Platía Dhiagoras to enter the town's second archaeological site.

7 ODEION AND ARCHAEOLOGICAL SITE

The lively mosaics and wall-paintings uncovered in the ruins of 3rd-century AD Roman houses are the main attraction of this site. Other highlights are the pillars of the ancient gymnasium and the beautifully restored Nymphaion, which dates from the 4th century BC.

With its mosaics, well and statues it was first thought by archaeologists to be a sanctuary to all the goddesses. Only later was it discovered to be a lavishly decorated public urinal!

Northeast Aegean Islands

*T*he islands of the northeast Aegean are more remote from Athens and further from each other than those of the cluttered southern waters.

Each has its own strong identity, and the region offers a rich choice of scenic splendours, from the verdant vineyards of Sámos to the rocky splendour of Mount Fengári on Samothráki and the treeless hills of Límnos.

Striking village architecture, broad landscapes and a wealth of medieval sights add to the highly individual charm of each island, and their long coastlines hide many of Greece's least-explored beaches.

Fertile farmlands make the larger northeastern isles prosperous – Sámos is famous for its wine and Lésvos (Lesbos) and Chíos are renowned for their ouzo. Life here has been less harsh than on less favoured islands.

The Turkish coast is never far off – it is within a few kilometres of Lésvos, Sámos and Chíos – and a strong military presence on several islands is a reminder of tensions between Greece and Turkey. Since oil was discovered beneath the ocean floor (Greece's only oil rig stands off Thásos), Turkey has renewed claims to mineral rights on the continental shelf. These claims are strenuously denied by Greece.

Memory of Turkish rule is recent, as the Northeast Aegean joined free Greece only in 1912, after Greek victory in the First Balkan War.

NORTHEAST AEGEAN ISLANDS

The 11th-century Néa Moní stands among cypress trees

The majority of the island's most interesting sights and its best beaches are in the southern half of the island, south and west of the capital, Chíos.
75km south of Lésvos.

CHÍOS TOWN (CHÓRA)

The capital is a busy commercial port and is not much concerned with tourism, though a handful of old streets and buildings lend it character.
Midway along the east coast, facing Turkey. East coast of Chíos.

Byzantino Moussío (Post-Byzantine Museum/Medjitie Djami)

The courtyard of this former mosque encloses a fascinating array of objects from green bronze cannons bearing Venetian crests to Jewish and Turkish tombstones.
Kanari 9, opposite public gardens. Open: Tuesday to Sunday 10am–1pm. Admission free.

Dimotikos Kipos (Public Gardens)

A ring of mature palms surrounds a pair of marble heraldic griffons and a heroic bronze statue of Konstantinos Kanaris (1822), one of the leaders of the War of Independence.
Town centre. Freely accessible.

Kástro (Castle)

The dilapidated walls of the castle quarter (now being restored in places) enclose tumbledown Turkish shop-houses of great charm. The turban-topped tombstones of a Turkish cemetery, shaded by palms, mark the corner of Odós Mit. Arseniou and Odós Tzon Kenenty (John Kennedy), while the

CHÍOS (KHIOS)

Chíos is a long, crescent island close to the Turkish coast. Its biggest attractions are in the high, rolling hinterland of the south, where a handful of unique fortified villages are hidden in fertile pockets among steep hillsides. The island has no outstanding ancient sites but it does possess a wealth of medieval survivals from a richly-textured past which blends Byzantine, Genoese, Venetian and Turkish influences.

A century of Venetian rule (1204–1304) was followed by the long reign of the Genoese Giustiniani family (1346–1566). The massacre of 30,000 islanders after a failed revolt in 1882 was immortalised by the French painter Eugène Delacroix (1798–1863) and hardened European support for Greece against the Turks.

clustered domes of a derelict medieval hammam (Turkish bath) may be seen built into the ramparts at the north end of Navarchos Nikodimou. Ringed by a now-dry moat, the castle was built in the 10th century AD by the Byzantines and added to by later conquerors.

West end of Neoreion, one block west of the waterfront. Freely accessible.

Moussío Philippou Argentis (Philip Argentis Museum)

A rich collection of etchings, drawings, traditional costumes and wooden furniture and utensils.

Korai 2, in the Bibliothiki Khiou Korai (Korai Library) (tel: 0 271 44246). Open: Monday to Thursday 8am–2pm, Friday 8am–2pm and 5.30–7.30pm; Saturday 8am–12.30pm. Admission charge.

MASTIKOKHORIA (MASTIC VILLAGES)

The mastic bush, which grows semi-wild all over southern Chíos, was the source of great wealth in medieval times and is still harvested for its gum, which is used as a base for sweets and perfumes and is claimed to have medicinal properties. The unique fortified Mastikokhoria are walled labyrinths, easy to defend against raiders.

35 to 45km southwest of Chíos Town.

MESTÁ

The best preserved 'mastic village' is a kasbah-like maze of warmly coloured stone alleyways and arches surrounding a lovely central square.

10km northwest of Pyrgí.

NÉA MONÍ (NEW MONASTERY)

The monastery, built in the 11th century by the Byzantine emperor, Constantine Monomachos, is the finest of its type in Greece. Its striking mosaics are its biggest attraction.

15km west of Chíos Town. Open: daily 6am–1pm and 4–8pm. Free.

OLÝMPOI

Olýmpoi has grown up around a 13th-century core of walls, with a 20m defensive tower in its central square. The arched gate of Kato Porta was originally the only way into the village.

5km northwest of Pyrgí.

PYRGÍ

Pyrgí's maze of alleys and tall balconied houses covered with elaborate, dazzling geometric designs called *xista* is striking. Clusters of tomatoes and peppers hung to dry from balconies add splashes of vermilion.

35km southwest of Chíos Town.

Geometric patterns and drying tomatoes outside a Pyrgí bakery

IKARÍA

Long, thin and very mountainous, Ikaría lies midway between green Sámos and chic Mýkonos (see Cyclades) and most island-hoppers bypass it on their way from one to the other. It's said to be where Ikaros, son of the legendary Minoan inventor Dedalos (Daedalus), plummeted to his death after flying too close to the sun, so melting the wax which held his newly-made wings together. Others who have landed here unwillingly include the composer of the ubiquitous theme tune from *Zorba the Greek*, Mikis Theodorakis, one of many left-wing dissidents confined to Ikaría by pre- and post-war dictatorships.

Ikaría's south coast looks like one long cliff, with its only anchorage at Ágios Kírykos, the island's main port and capital, at its east end. The north coast is almost equally rugged, but the cliffs are broken by deltas of farmland at the mouths of steep valleys. The extensive pine woodlands of Ikaría's inland plateau have been badly damaged by fire, but the island hinterland is surprisingly verdant. Like Sámos, it is watered by small year-round streams.
30km east of Sámos; 50km west of Mýkonos.

ÁGIOS KÍRYKOS

Ikaría's capital is a sleepy village of tumbledown houses overlooking a fishing harbour and a little-used ferry port.
East end of the south coast.

ARMENISTÍS

A fishing hamlet and a row of tavernas overlook a north-facing bay and the best beaches on the island, two long stretches of coarse white sand.
57km west of Ágios Kírykos.

ÉVDILOS

The island's second port is near-derelict but coming back to life thanks to foreign and domestic tourism.
46km northwest of Ágios Kírykos.

NAS

Nas is little more than a name on the map: three tavernas cater for campers and sunbathers on the (unofficial) nude beach in a pebbly, cliff-ringed cove.
4km west of Armenistís.

Naós Artemis Tavropoliou (Sanctuary of Artemis of the Bulls)

The impressive stepped foundations of this temple overlook a reed-fringed freshwater pool.
Immediately above the beach at Nas. Freely accessible.

Quayside at Ágios Kírykos

LÍMNOS (LEMNOS)

The rolling hills of Límnos are treeless and covered with a golden fuzz of pasture and grain fields. It's one of the richest agricultural islands, and the round stone towers of derelict windmills are dotted around fields where sturdy grey cattle graze.

Though relatively undiscovered, Límnos has some fine beaches around its rocky shores

Órmos Moúdrou (Moudros Bay) takes a huge bite out of the south coast. This vast, well-sheltered natural harbour made Límnos a strategic base for the British fleet during the Gallipoli campaign of 1915, for the Turkish coast and the Dardanelles are only 60km to the east. For the same reason, Límnos remains highly militarised, with Greek army and navy installations on most of its hilltops and anchorages.

75km northwest of Lésvos; 270km northeast of Píreas.

MÝRINA

The island's cheerfully old-fashioned but well-kept main town is guarded by a Venetian castle and has two accessible beaches. A narrow, flagstoned main street runs from Platía Oktobríou 8, next to the harbour, through the bazaar-like shopping area, lined with charming old-fashioned shop-houses with sagging tiled roofs and heavy shutters.

Arkheologiko Moussío (Archaeological Museum)

Stone-Age and Bronze-Age finds from sites around the island.

On the Romaikos beach-front 1km west of the harbour. Open: Tuesday to Sunday 8.30am–3pm. Admission charge.

Frourio Nepheli (Nepheli Castle)

A 13th-century Venetian castle with towers and battlements still intact, is dramatically located on a crag. A semi-wild flock of fallow deer roam its slopes.

500m west of harbour. Open: hours of daylight. Admission free.

Romaikos Yialos

Mýrina's main beach offers a 1.5km stretch of clean, coarse sand, lined with cafés.

500m to 1.5km from the harbour, north of the castle.

POLYÓCHNI

Traces of one of the oldest settlements in Greece, dating from the fourth millennium BC, are clearly visible and well described by explanatory signs.

33km east of Mýrina, 3km east of Kaminia village (signposted). Open: daylight hours. Admission free.

LÉSVOS (LESBOS)

Lésvos, the third largest of all the Greek islands and one of the most populous – with 105,000 people in its 1,630sq km – has a bit of everything. There are fine beaches on its 370km-long coastline, some of them busy, others quite deserted. There are rolling, olive-covered hills and pastoral lowlands, arid semi-desert landscapes interspersed by oasis-like valleys and bald summits emerging from pine-forested foothills. There are quiet fishing harbours, even quieter farming villages in the hills, and one breathtakingly pretty historic town turned resort. It even has its own 'sea', the mirror-calm Kólpos Kallonís, which plunges deeply into the southern coastline. There are some 11 million olive trees, and road verges are often lined with yellow clusters of aniseed, a reminder that Lésvos produces some of Greece's best ouzo.

75km southeast of Límnos; 240km northeast of Athens.

MÍTHYMNA (MÓLIVOS)

A delightful, charmingly preserved village of pink and grey stone mansions with bright red, green, yellow and blue woodwork ascends to the battlements and circular bastions of the Genoese castle – a dramatic sight when floodlit at night. A pebble-and-sand beach runs along the bay east of the village, and fishing boats bob in the small, taverna-ringed harbour.

62km northwest of Mytilíni.

Eressos Arkheologiko Moussío (Archaeological Museum)

This clearly described collection of finds includes charming pottery heads and figurines, barnacle-encrusted clay jars recovered from the seabed and fascinating original photographs depicting the arrival of the Greek forces in 1912.

In the Dhimotikon (Town Hall). Signposted (tel: 0251 22087) Open: Tuesday to Sunday 8.30am–3pm.
Admission charge.

Frourio Molyvou (Mólivos Castle)

From the battlements there are fine views of the village, the surrounding hills and farmland, and the nearby Turkish coast.

Above the village. Open: Tuesday to Sunday 7.30am–8pm. Admission free.

MONÍ YPSILOU (IPSILO MONASTERY)

A fortified eyrie, dedicated to Áyios Ioannis Theológos (St John the Divine). Arcaded cells surround a cobbled courtyard and church and its walls are partly decorated with bright blue tiles. A small museum on the second floor displays gorgeous embroidered vestments and illustrated manuscripts.

80km west of Mytilíni on the road to Sígri. Open: daily. Admission free for museum.

MONÍ LEIMONOS (LIMONOS MONASTERY)

Constructed in 1527, this is a graceful, rambling building of decorative brick cloisters and grey and pink stone. Its three-room museum displays embroidered robes and crowns, jewellery, icons and reliquaries.

45km west of Mytilíni, 400m south of main east–west road. Open: 9am–1pm and 5–7.30pm. Admission charge for museum.

MYTILÍNI

The island capital is a commercial centre with a population of 25,000. Its visitor appeal is three-pronged – a bustling,

Tall 19th-century buildings overlook Mytilíni's long sweep of waterfront

eastern-flavoured bazaar area along Odós Ermou, an impressive stronghold, and several excellent museums.

Arkheologiko Moussío (Archaeological Museum)

Statues, pottery and other finds from local sites.
South end of 8 Novembriou (tel: 0251 22087) Open: daily 8.30am–3pm. Admission charge.

Kástro (Castle)

Reconstructed by the Genoese Gattelusi family in 1373, crumbling walls surround the hilltop crowned by massive round towers.
On the eastern promontory, north of the ferry harbour. Open: Monday to Friday 7.30am–3pm. Admission charge.

Moussío Laiki Texnis (Museum of Popular Art)

Village costumes and other memorabilia in a charmingly-restored former harbourmaster's office.
Platía Sapphous, on the waterfront. Open: daily summer only 10am–1pm. Admission charge.

Moussío Theophilou (Theophilos Museum)

The self-taught naïve painter Theophilos (1873–1934), born on Lésvos, wandered Greece painting for his dinner. The collection includes more than 80 of his charming paintings of landscapes and scenes from mythology, folklore and village life.
4km from the town centre in Varia suburb. Signposted (tel:0 251 28179). Open: Tuesday to Sunday, 8.30am–3pm and 4.30–8pm. Admission charge.

PÉTRA

A long, coarse-sand beach and small resort popular for its proximity to Míthymna.
5km south of Míthymna.

SKÁLA ERESOÚ (ERESSOS)

A small resort on the island's best beach, backed by harsh mountains and an oasis-like delta of fertile farmland.
92km southwest of Mytilíni.

Sámos

Sámos is the most popular holiday island in the Northeast Aegean and one of Greece's most startlingly beautiful islands. To anyone arriving from the stark, arid landscapes of the Cyclades or the Dodecanese, Sámos is strikingly verdant, with dark green cypress spires rising from slopes covered with poplars, plane-trees and creepers. Limestone crags emerge from thickly wooded slopes so that Samian scenery looks like the work of a 19th-century Romantic landscape painter.

Set among this natural beauty are prosperous villages which, with their red tiles, white walls and square stone-built bell-towers, could be in Italy. The island's abundant greenery owes much to its geology: streams and springs emerge from its granite rock to water the vineyards which account for much of the island's income, and Samaina, the dry white wine made by the Cooperative des Vinicoles de Sámos (Sámos Viticulturists' Cooperative) is perhaps the only Greek wine which will bear international comparison.

In antiquity, and especially under the rule of Polykrates (c536–522BC), Sámos was a great naval power. It entered the 'tourism' business early, for it was already a popular holiday destination in the Roman era of the second and first centuries BC. After rule by the Byzantines, Franks, Venetians and Genoese, it fell to the Turks in 1475 and despite gaining limited self-rule after 1832, as an autonomous principality within the Ottoman Empire, it did not join Greece until 1912.

Surprisingly, Sámos has little to show for its glorious and exciting past. Its charm lies in its landscapes and in its beaches, which include lovely stretches of dazzling white pebbles on the north coast and some excellent sandy strands on the east and south shores. *210km east of Píreas.*

SÁMOS

ÁGIOS KONSTANTÍNOS

A leafy Italianate village spread out along several kilometres of pebble beach on the main north coast road, Ágios Konstantínos is far less developed than nearby Kokkári and the starting point for exploring the cypress-covered slopes and network of paths inland (see pages 128–9).

Midway along the north coast.

IRAÍO

The white fluted column of the Temple to Hera marks both the island's most important classical site and the tiny, newly-built resort which has sprung up on the pebbly bay next to it.

13km southwest of Pythagóreio.

Naós Iraío (Temple of Hera)

This site is extremely old, with evidence of Mycenaean-era settlement as early as the second millennium BC. The lone column of the great 23m-high temple devoted to Hera, wife of Zeus, is undeniably striking, but the site is confusing and there are no descriptive signs to help you make sense of it.

500m east of the modern village of Iraío (tel: 0273 61177). Open: Tuesday to Sunday 8.30am–3pm. Admission charge. May be closed for further excavation.

KERKETÉFS ÓROS (MOUNT KERKIS)

At 1,433m, this is one of the highest peaks in the Aegean and its bald dome dominates all of western Sámos. Keen walkers can follow the challenging steep track from the south coast road to the summit.

West end of Sámos; summit track signposted to Evangelístria from the coast road west of Votsalákia.

KOKKÁRI

A delightfully picturesque fishing village-cum-resort, immediately recognisable from scores of postcards and holiday brochures. There are pebbly beaches and coves to the west of the village.

20km west of Vathí, on the north coast.

The small castle at Pythagóreio overlooks the sea

N KARLOVÁSI

The island's sprawling western port and commercial centre has few sights of note, though two snarling Venetian marble lions stand in its public gardens, near the town centre. Karlovási's main importance from the visitor's point of view is as an arrival and departure point for island-hopping.

45km west of Vathí, on the north coast.

ÓRMOS MARATHÓKAMPOS

This pleasant, peaceful village has a thriving boat-building industry which turns out traditionally-built wooden caïques for local fishermen. It lies at the west end of a long, almost-deserted bay with pebbly beaches. To the west looms the often cloud-capped summit of Kerketéfs.

20km south of Karlovási.

PSILÍ ÁMMOS

Confusingly, Sámos has two beaches by this name. Both are excellent, sandy bays. **Psilí Ámmos (west)** is the less crowded, with almost a kilometre of fine sand, facing south.

5km west of Órmos Marathókampos.

Psilí Ámmos (east) is around 400m of sand, usually invisible beneath dozens of sunbathing bodies.

8km northeast of Pythagóreio.

PYTHAGÓREIO

The third of Sámos's three ports is only 10km from the Turkish coast and the departure point for day trips to the Turkish resort of Kusadasi. Tavernas cluster the quayside of an enormous harbour where yachts outnumber fishing boats. The remnants of the 6th-century BC city walls can be seen curving around the harbour and the hills behind the

village. These are almost the only indication that this is the site of the great ancient city of Sámos. Pythagóreio has been so named since 1955, after Pythagoras, the Classical-era mathematician who formulated the famous theorem that the square of the hypotenuse of a right angled triangle is equal to the sum of the squares on the other two sides. Born here in the 6th century BC, and a protégé of the tyrant Polykrates, he later emigrated to the Greek colonies in southern Italy.

Southeast corner of Sámos.

Arkheologiko Moussío (Archaeological Museum)

Finds from the Iraío site (see page 121) include busts of Roman emperors and a 1st-century BC statue of Augustus Caesar.

In village hall (tel: 0273 61400). Open: Tuesday to Sunday 8.30am–3pm. Admission free.

Kástro (Castle of Lykurgos Logothetes)

This miniature castle was built in 1824 by the leader of the island's rebellion against the Turks. Around it are the remains of colonnaded houses from the Roman era.

In the centre of the village, 400m west of the harbour. Freely accessible.

SAMIOPOÚLA

The uninhabited islet of Samiopoúla nestles close to its parent island. Covered in pines and with several pretty pebbly coves for swimming and sunbathing, it is a pleasant destination for swimming and snorkelling trips, organised by boat operators from Pythagóreio and Órmos Marathókampos.

5km south of Órmos Marathókampos.

Above: Sámos has the most wooded landscapes in the Aegean islands; right: Vourliótes, high in the Sámos Hills, attracts walkers

VATHÍ

The island's capital straddles a long inlet at the eastern end of the north coast. Built in the 19th century, its neo-classical buildings with their grandiose façades and the fountain and palm trees in the waterfront *platía* have a certain faded elegance.

Arkheologiko Moussío (Archaeological Museum)

This houses the largest known free-standing Greek statue, a 5m-tall figure of a youth, apparently dedicated to Apollo, excavated at the Iraío site. The cauldrons decorated with bronze griffons on display here are unique to Sámos.

In the square at the east end of Kapetan Katavani (tel: 0273 27469). Open: Tuesday to Sunday 8.30am–3pm, Monday 11am–5pm. Admission charge.

Byzantino Moussío (Byzantine Museum)

An assortment of icons, chalices, holy vessels, bones of saints and parchment manuscripts are on display here.

In the Mitropoli (Cathedral), one block back from the waterfront, between Asklipiadou and 28 Oktobriou. Open: Tuesday to Sunday 8.30am–3pm. Admission charge.

Dimotiki Pinakothiki (Municipal Art Gallery)

Collection of portraits of grandly-dressed princes of 19th-century Sámos and bewhiskered heroes of the War of Independence (1821–30).

Above the post office in the square at the east end of Kapetan Katavani, next to the Town Hall. Open: daily 8am–3pm. Admission free.

SAMOTHRÁKI

The egg-shaped isle of Samothráki rises to the central peak of Mount Fengári, the highest mountain in the Aegean islands at 1,611m. On its lower northern slopes lies fertile farmland where almost all the island's people work and live. The grain fields, sheep-folds and thick woodland of this well-watered north coast are in sharp contrast to the jagged shapes of Fengári's peaks and the near-desert wilderness of the southeast of the island.
45km south of the mainland port of Alexandroúpoli.

KAMARIÓTISSA

The island's main village is close to its western tip. Ferries and hydrofoils link Samothráki to the mainland and to the isles to the north and south.
Close to the western tip of the island.

PALAIÓPOLI

The site of the island's original capital, abandoned in the post-Byzantine period, and now the location of the most impressive archaeological site in the Northeast Aegean.

Ieron ton Megalon Theon (Sanctuary of the Great Gods)

The huge hillside site is second only to the Minoan sites on Crete for sheer impact. High points include the plinth of the Rotunda of Arsinoe and the five surviving columns of the Hieron, plus remnants of the theatre, the sanctuary's massive fortifications and other shrines.
6km northeast of Kamariótissa, signposted to Archaeological Museum from coast road. Open: Tuesday to Sunday 8.30am–3pm. Admission charge.

Moussío Arkaeologiko (Archaeological Museum)

Finds from the site include: altars and friezes; votive offerings; lovely delicate Roman glassware and tinsel-like gold jewellery; 5th-century BC black-figure pottery columns from the Rotunda of Arsinoe and a replica of the Winged Victory of Samothráki (the original was removed by French archaeologists in 1863 and is now in the Louvre, Paris).
6km northeast of Kamariótissa, signposted from coast road. Open: same hours and admission charge as site.

SAMOTHRÁKI TOWN (CHÓRA)

Samothráki's tiny medieval capital is at the head of a hidden valley on the lower slopes of the island's central massif. It is a pretty jumble of two-storey white stone houses with painted shutters and red-tiled roofs, crowned by a small, ruined Byzantine-Genoese castle.
5km from Kamariótissa.

Kástro (Castle)

Round and square bastions surround a tiny square inner keep with a beautiful view down into a wooded valley to the sea and over to the coast of Thrace (Thráki) on the mainland. Marble slabs carved with Byzantine inscriptions and heraldic devices decorate the walls. The lower storey is the police station.
On the crag above the village. Freely accessible.

Laografiko Moussío (Folk Museum)

Old-time implements include a wooden loom and spinning wheel, pottery and some vividly coloured embroideries.
Above the public library, by the main square and immediately below the Church of the Virgin. Open: daily, 9am–1pm and 7–9pm. Admission charge.

THE CULT OF THE GREAT GODS

The colonists from Sámos who arrived on Samothráki around 700BC found the island already settled by earlier people with their own religion. The Samians absorbed the local gods into their own pantheon to create the hybrid cult of the Great Gods, building a vast sanctuary as their place of worship. The cult survived for almost a millennium, remaining popular well into Roman times, partly because unlike other mystery religions of the time it was open to women and slaves as well as the ruling class. Its pantheon descended from pre-Greek Thracian fertility deities and included the Great Mother, a consort named Kadmilos, and two enigmatic intercessor gods, the Kabiroi, who were later identified with the Dioscouri of the Classical Greek pantheon.

Marble columns stand above the Sanctuary of the Great Gods

Naós tis Kimisis (Church of the Virgin)

This enormous whitewashed church, built in 1875, houses the skulls of the Five Martyrs of Samothráki, early Christian saints of the Orthodox faith.
Centre of village. If closed inquire at the public library next door for keys.

Thásos is picturesque and little-visited

THÁSOS (THASSOS)

A circular island of low hills and gentle valleys, Thásos is one of Greece's greener isles – though not as green as it once was. Its pine forests are only now recovering from forest fires which struck in the 1980s, and many of its slopes, especially those on the west side of the island, are cloaked in young newly planted trees. A single road makes a 100km circuit round Thásos, with giddying switchbacks through the hills of the east coast.

Thásos has a couple of quiet resorts and one outstanding beach, but hasn't yet been discovered by tourism in a big way, despite the fact that international charter flights bring package tourists to mainland Kavála, a mere 30-minute ferry hop away.
25km southeast of mainland port of Kavála.

ALYKÍ
This delightful one-time fishing hamlet is no more than a row of white cottages roofed with slabs of grey stone. It sits on a tiny isthmus leading to a pine-covered headland, with a tiny sandy beach on its west side and a clear bay and a pebbly beach on its east flank.
52km south of Thásos Town by road.

Sanctuary of the Dioscuri
Column stumps, walls and foundations, and a stone sarcophagus mark this 7th-century BC site. On the headland immediately above are the ruins of two 5th-century AD Christian churches.
Signposted, 50m west of the village. Freely accessible.

CHRYSÍ AMMOUDIÁ
This gorgeous sweep of coarse white sand and clear water is ringed by dramatic, pine-clad limestone cliffs rising towards the 1,204m peak of Ypsário and the 1,100m summit of Profitis Ilías. The small resort of Chrysí Ammoudiá is at the north end of the beach, with a gaggle of tavernas and houses.

Another resort, Skála Potamias, lies at the south end.
7 to 9km from Thásos Town.

International Symposium for Marble Sculpture
A surprising collection of modern abstract sculpture sitting among the dunes includes a striking white totem-pole, a mirror-mosaic cube and a glass-studded pyramid.
At the north end of Chrysí Ammoudiá beach. Freely accessible.

LIMENÁRIA
The island's biggest holiday resort, comprising a clutter of shops, tavernas

and small hotels, along a sandy bay on the south coast.
55km south of Thásos Town.

THÁSOS TOWN (LIMENAS)

Thásos Town, the island capital, sits on a double bay facing the mainland (at its nearest only 11km away) with a deep modern ferry harbour and a shallow old harbour. This pleasant, sleepy modern town is ringed by ancient walls, overlooked by a medieval castle, and dotted with striking Hellenistic remains. The massive walls of ancient Thásos date from 495BC and form a 2km hilltop ring around Limin.
(Note: don't confuse Limenas with Limenária, see opposite).
North coast of Thásos.

Agion Apostolon (Holy Apostles)

A small modern whitewashed church stands amid the ruins and columns of an early Christian basilica, itself built from remnants of a pre-Christian shrine.
On the headland above the boatyard, 500m east of the old harbour. Freely accessible.

Agorá (Ancient Agorá)

The grand ground plan of Hellenistic (3rd to 1st century BC) Thásos can clearly be seen, with column bases marking the arcades of the great stoas and other buildings.
By the old harbour. Open: Tuesday to Friday 8am–7pm, weekends 8.30am–3pm. Admission charge.

Arkheologiko Moussío (Archaeological Museum)

This fine collection includes a sculpture – the Kriophoros of Thásos, a giant archaic statue, dating from the 6th century BC, of a naked youth carrying a ram to sacrifice, terracotta works, and marble and ivory carvings.
Next to the agorá. Open: Tuesday to Friday 8am–7pm, weekends 8.30am–3pm. Admission charge.

Arkheo Theatro (Ancient Theatre)

This marble-tiered theatre is still used in summer when music and drama performances take advantage of the perfect acoustics.
750m above the agorá. Freely accessible.

Kástro (Castle)

The battlements of a medieval Genoese castle surmount the city walls at their highest point.
1km west of Agion Apostolon, 250m from Arkheo Theatro. Freely accessible.

The ancient theatre at Thásos Town, used for performances in the summer

Hills of Sámos

The hills rising from the north coast of the island combine verdant woodlands with dramatic mountain views and quaint villages. This walk starts and finishes on the coast, and if you start by 9am you should arrive back in Kokkári in time for lunch and a lazy afternoon on the beach.

The route may be slightly altered by newly-built dirt roads; the walking path is marked with red dots painted on walls and boulders, but you must keep a sharp eye open for these. *Allow 3–4 hours.*

Start at the southwest end of Kokkári, at the junction of the old road through the village and the new bypass, next to the Míos Beach Hotel. Follow the tarred side road which quickly turns into a dirt track, and keep left of the farm fields, inland of Kokkári until after 10 minutes the track – now a footpath – passes under a derelict Turkish aqueduct. Continue to follow this trail, crossing two new forestry jeep tracks.

1 TSAMADOU

The trail follows the 200m contour, with the vivid turquoise bay of Tsamadou and its white pebble beach immediately below, to your right.

Continue across a rocky ravine to the base of the final pitch to Vourliótes village.

2 KALDERIMI

The last, and steepest stage of the walk follows one of Sámos's surviving *kalderimia*, the painstakingly cobbled mule-paths which once criss-crossed every island but which have been destroyed in many places by new road-building or have simply been neglected.

After 90 minutes the trail meets the tarred road to Vourliótes. Continue for a further 15 minutes to the village.

3 VOURLIÓTES

The outskirts of Vourliótes are reminiscent of a ghost town, with the tumbledown walls of abandoned houses lining narrow lanes. In the last century the village had 1,200 inhabitants. It now has fewer than half that number, but

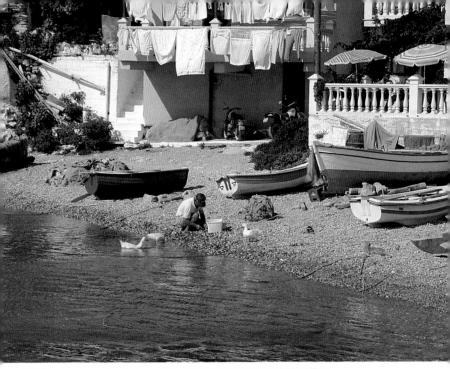

Kokkári, where the walk ends, is a quaint combination of resort and fishing village

streams and fertile land make the remaining inhabitants prosperous by hill-village standards.

Stop for a drink and snack in the quaint central square.

Return to Kokkári via the Moní Vrontá trail, rising to 500m above sea level. Head south on the track (signposted and marked with red dots) which leads from the eastern corner of Vourliótes.

4 MONÍ VRONTÁ (OUR LADY OF THE THUNDER)

The substantial, stone-roofed monastery of Vrontá dates from the 16th century, when Sámos – which had been deserted for a century because of pirate raids – was resettled by Greeks from Asia Minor under a benevolent pasha. According to island belief, thunderstorms always follow the festival of the Birth of the Virgin which is celebrated here and in Vourliótes in lively fashion on 7–8 September each year.

(Note: the Greek army sometimes billets troops in the monastery, and photography may be banned if they are in residence.)

From Vrontá follow the path downhill and northeast from the monastery, signposted Monopati Kokkári (Kokkárivia Footpath) in Greek. The trail follows the right bank of a deep gorge, with sheer cliffs on the opposite side and views down to Kokkári. On a clear day you can see right across to Turkey.

After another 45 minutes the trail cuts across a web of fields and dirt tracks, passes through olive groves, and emerges at a taverna on the main road, 500m from Kokkári village centre.

FISHERMEN AND BOATBUILDERS

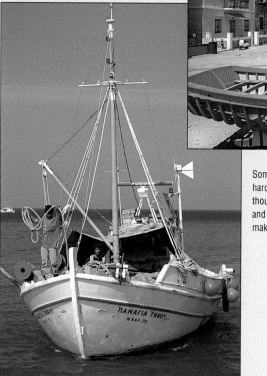

Old gnarled cross-legged fishermen mending bright yellow or dark crimson nets are one of the everyday sights of the Greek islands, and no island harbour is complete without its flotilla of tiny, brightly painted fishing boats.

Almost all of them bear the names of a local saint, who protects both boat and boatmen. This is a very traditional form of life insurance, and is reflected onshore in the tiny chapels dedicated to the Panagía (Virgin), built by grateful fishermen in thanks for their safekeeping and livelihood at sea.

You can see traditional wooden caïques being built and repaired at the harbours of Kokkári and Karlovási on Sámos

Some things hardly change, though engines and nylon nets make life easier of nets. The sound of their engines 'putt-putting' back into harbour at first light starts many an island day.

Another oft-heard harbour sound is the slap of an octopus being tenderised by pounding its rubbery tentacles against a boulder. Octopus are taken with a trident or a formidable triple hook on a handline.

On most islands the catch is as small as the boats. Overfishing has taken its toll of Aegean stocks. Island boatmen pursue their quarry with everything from fine-mesh nets to spear-guns and fish-traps. Dynamite was sometimes used to maximise results, and it is not uncommon to meet an older fisherman who has lost a hand through mishandling explosives. These days, more environmentally friendly fish farms are widely established in an effort to increase island fish stocks.

(see pages 120–2), Sými (page 154), Thásos Town (Limenas) on Thásos (page 127) and at other island ports.

If you look closely at the prow of one of these little vessels you will often see a diamond-shape cut into the wood – a stylised version of the eye painted on the prow of the ancient triremes and a reminder that the captains of these little fishing-boats are descendants of the sailors who trounced the Persian fleet at Salamis.

Tourism, and increasing prosperity in Greece itself, have played a part in encouraging intensive fishing. Greeks and tourists love fresh fish, and prices for the prized *barbounia* (red mullet) have soared.

Much fishing is done at night. Flotillas of dinghies, each carrying a pair of powerful gas lamps, are used to attract squid and small fry into circles

Finally, on island beaches you may see fishermen of another sort: young romeos who spend their summers in pursuit of female tourists are called *kamaki* – 'harpooners'.

Sporádes and Évvoia (Evia)

*T*he gentle, pine-cloaked Sporádes with their mild summers, superb beaches and postcard-pretty villages are easy to fall in love with at first sight. An archipelago of rocky, uninhabited islets lies around the four main isles, each of which has a distinct character of its own.

Three of the four Sporádes islands – Skíathos, Skópelos and Alónnisos – are within sight of each other and connected by a fast hydrofoil service which also

SPORÁDES AND ÉVVOIA

links them with the port of Vólos within the Pagasitikós Kólpos (Pagasitic Gulf) on the mainland. The fourth, Skýros, is far to the southeast, off the eastern shore of the wooded fertile island of Évvoia which lies parallel to the mainland coast and within a few kilometres of the mainland for its entire length.

The four Sporádes have just enough visitable history to make them interesting, with a deserted secret village here, or a medieval monastery or Venetian fortification, there. Their real appeal is, however, their idyllic beaches, gentle landscapes and relative lack of mass-market tourism.

Skíathos, with an international airport, is the busiest, but out of the peak holiday season its dozens of sandy beaches offer enough space for everyone. Skópelos has only recently been discovered by the holiday industry, while Alónnisos, Skýros and Évvoia remain well off the beaten track.

Above: the fertile farmlands of Évvoia are a chequerboard of grain fields and olive groves
Below: Skýros Town stands below a rocky crag crowned by a fortified monastery

ALÓNNISOS

Alónnisos is the quietest and remotest of the three western Sporádes. Hillier, and less greenly forested than its neighbours, it is also the most sparsely inhabited isle. In 1965, an earthquake rocked its main village and the islanders relocated to Patitíri, now the island's harbour and main centre. Much of the coast is lined with steep, eye-catching cliffs, and its scatttering of beaches – some sandy, some pebbly, none crowded – are best approached by boat. In summer, small craft ply several times a day from Patitíri, saving a long, hot trek.

A Byzantine shipwreck has been found on the seabed near the island, and the rare Mediterranean monk seal lives around the uninhabited islets north of Alónnisos. As a result the waters north of the island have been declared a marine conservation area, and we would urge

you to boycott trips to sea caves which may be used by the seals (see page 156). *25km east of Skíathos.*

ALÓNNISOS TOWN (CHÓRA)

Abandoned after the earthquake, when the government relocated its inhabitants to Patitíri, this delightfully pretty village is coming back to life, mainly as a result of its charming but derelict houses being bought by Athenians and foreigners who restore them as holiday homes. Islanders are outnumbered by English and German residents, and Alónnisos Town really only comes to life in July and August.
Inland of the west coast, close to the southern point of the island.

KALAMAKIA

A long stretch of pebbly and sandy beach with several small seasonal tavernas.
East coast, 8km north of Patitíri.

KOKKINOKÁSTRO

A lovely pebble beach, surrounded by hills, cliffs and pinewoods, Kokkinokástro has been identified as the site of the oldest prehistoric settlement in the Aegean islands and excavations have located the remains of ancient Ikos. The site is of more interest to archaeologists than casual sightseers. Diligent searching reveals the stumps of a short stretch of the city wall near the beach.
East coast, 5km north of Patitíri (unmarked) and freely accessible.

PATITÍRI

Patitíri is a modern settlement, thrown up in a hurry to rehouse villagers from Chóra after the 1965 quake. Since then, the Greek islanders' passion for flowers, pot plants, greenery and idiosyncratic decorations of all sorts has done much to

---

THE CYCLOPS

The deserted island of Gioúra, 25km north of Alónnisos, was said to be the home of the Cyclops, the cannibalistic one-eyed giants of Greek mythology. In Homer's epic, The Odyssey, one of them, Polyphemus, captured the wandering Odysseus and his crew on their long journey home from the siege of Troy. After Polyphemus had seized and eaten several of his men, Odysseus blinded the monster with a sharpened stake, then craftily escaped from the cave tied beneath the bellies of the Cyclops' sheep. In his rage, Polyphemus hurled huge boulders after Odysseus' departing ship, thus forming the craggy reefs and islets around Gioúra.

Many of the pretty houses in old Alónnisos Town have been renovated as holiday homes

personalise the once-charmless settlement. Its location, on a calm bay hemmed in by low sandstone bluffs and pine-wooded hillsides, is hard to beat.

A gradually-decaying *kalderimi* (cobbled donkey path) leads up a pretty 45-minute hike to Alónnisos Town, situated on the hills above.

East coast, close to the southern end of the island.

PERISTÉRA

Separated by a narrow strait from Alónnisos, the tiny isle of Peristéra is at times busier than its big sister. In high season, its beaches are a popular destination for day-trips from Skópelos and even from Skíathos. At other times, its hamlets, Peristéra, in the south, and Livádia, an anchorage on the west coast, are usually deserted and then the island is only for the most demanding of solitude-seekers.

10km northeast of Patitíri.

ÉVVOIA (EUBOEA, EVIA)

Some say Greece's second largest island (after Crete) hardly qualifies as an island at all. The Gulf of Évvoia (Evvoïkos Kólpos), which separates it from the mainland, narrows to a channel just 100m wide, and you can cross to the mainland by a swing-bridge. It is therefore not surprising that in some ways Évvoia's atmosphere is more akin to that of the mainland than to its nearest island neighbours.

Holidaymakers looking for the quick island fix offered by the smaller isles will not find Évvoia instantly charming, but explorers who take the time to discover it will not go away disappointed.

Inland, Évvoia is a fertile island of wide valleys and thickly wooded hills

The stone battlements of Castle Rosso loom over Kárystos harbour

cloaked in plane and chestnut trees. Beaches on its southwest coast, closest to Athens, are popular resorts for Greek holidaymakers from the mainland. In the north, the Greek fondness for thermal springs has encouraged the growth of several small beach-and-spa resorts. By contrast, the island's steep east coast is dotted with undiscovered beaches and coves, many of them accessible only by boat or by four-wheel-drive vehicle and strictly for self-sufficient beachcombers, as they are without facilities of any kind.

CHALKÍDA (KHALKIS)

Chalkída, the island's capital, was important in antiquity, when it controlled the main coastal shipping route from northern to southern Greece, and the whole island was one of the richest Venetian possessions in Greece until its fall to the Turks in 1470.

Today, few visitors linger in this

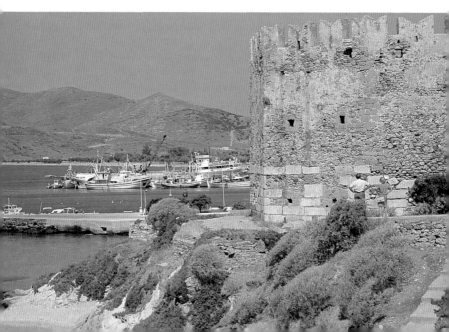

modern grimy industrial town for more time than it takes to check out its single natural wonder and visit its medieval stronghold.

West coast of Évvoia, 88km from Athens.

Evrípou

A swing-bridge carries the road across the Evripos strait which separates Évvoia from the mainland. Through this narrow channel swirls a current which changes direction several times a day for reasons which baffled Aristotle (who is said to have plunged into it in frustration), and continues to puzzle scientists even today.

Town centre.

Frourio Karababas (Karababa Fortress)

A grim 17th-century fortress, built by the Turks to control the narrows.

Hilltop on the island side of the Evripos bridge, north of road. Freely accessible.

DÝSTOS

Above the 5th-century BC ruins a small Venetian castle crowns a low hill where the acropolis of the ancient city stood.

By the shores of a marshy lake 5km south of Krieza, signposted, reached by dirt road from main Chalkída–Kárystos road. Freely accessible.

ERÉTRIA

In ancient times an important ally of Athens against the Persians, much of Erétria is concealed beneath the modern village.

21km southeast of Chalkída.

Arkheologiko Moussío (Archaeological Museum)

Pottery finds and bronzes from the site of ancient Erétria.

See Theatrou, below, for location and hours.

The Venetian-Greek church of Agía Paraskevi stands in the middle of Chalkída

Theatrou (Ancient Theatre)

Steps from the theatre descend to a vault below, while beside it are the foundations of a sanctuary and gymnasium.

Northwest part of village, signposted (tel: 0221 62206). Open: Tuesday to Sunday 8.30am–3pm. Combined admission charge for museum and site.

KÁRYSTOS

This is the main port for southern Évvoia and is a popular summer resort used by mainland Greeks. It has a long sand and shingle beach west of the town and is overlooked by the fine mountain scenery of Mount Ochi (Óros Óchi).

90km southeast of Chalkída.

Kástro (Castle Rosso)

The towering, wind-worn battlements of the great, empty castle, built by the Venetians in the 13th century, are an impressive sight on the low hill behind the town. It was once called Castello Rosso (Red Castle) for the dark red stone used in its turrets and walls.

1.5km from Kárystos harbour. Freely accessible.

SKÍATHOS

Skíathos claims to possess more and better beaches than any other Greek island. The claim is hard to argue with: not only are there enough beaches to give each of its many high-season visitors a fair share of space, but the beaches are made of the finest yellow sand in the Aegean.

Lined with nodding calamus reeds ('Greek bamboo'), and surrounded by pines which scent the island air, these are strands to delight the most demanding beach enthusiast.

The island's popularity is enhanced by an international airport which brings package holidaymakers from northern Europe, and Skíathos is also a popular resort for well-off Athenian villa- and yacht-owners.

All but a few hundred of the island's 4,000 inhabitants live in the only village, called either Skiathos Town or Chóra, but most visitors stay in one of the half-dozen resorts scattered around its 44km of coast.

Unimportant in ancient times, Skíathos passed from the Byzantines to the Venetians in the 13th century, then to the Turks in 1538, before rejoining Greece in 1828. Sightseeing includes pretty hillside monasteries on Skíathos itself, and there are boat and hydrofoil trips to the beautiful Pílion peninsula or the port of Vólos on the mainland and to the neighbouring islands of the Sporádes group (see pages 134–5, 140–3).
64km southeast of mainland port of Vólos.

KÁSTRO

The towering walls and drawbridge of the island's one-time main village defied seaborne raiders from the beginning of the 16th century until 1830, when, with the end of the War of Independence, the

islanders felt secure enough to move from their safe, but inconvenient clifftop homes, to build a new capital at Chóra. The medieval village had 22 churches and about 300 homes. Today just two churches survive.
8km northwest of Skíathos Town, access on foot or by boat.

Pantokrátor (Church of Christ)

This 17th-century church, contains some lovely Byzantine icons and frescos and a carved iconostasis (icon stand).
Within the walls of the Kástro; open irregularly.

KOUKOUNARIÉS

This is the longest beach on Skíathos and its top holiday destination, with several large and many small hotels. Koukounariés offers 1,000m of pine-shaded sand, watersports and all the accoutrements of a successful resort.
12km southwest of Skíathos Town.

LALARIA

A curved beach of white pebbles is hemmed in by white cliffs half way along the island's north coast. Undeveloped as yet, Lalaria receives a daily seaborne invasion of day-trippers from Koukounariés and Chóra.
8km north of Skíathos Town, access by boat or dirt road.

PANAGÍA EVANGELISTRÍAS

Built in the late 18th century, this monastery is best known for its striking frescos, which date from 1822.
4km north of Skíathos Town. Open: daily 8am–noon and 5–8pm. Admission free.

PANAGÍA KOUNÍSTRAS

This modest little monastery, founded in 1540 and restored in 1738, has glowing

Bourtzi island in Skíathos harbour was fortified by the Venetians

Byzantine icons and frescos.
6km west of Skíathos Town. Open: daily 8am–1pm and 5–8pm. Admission charge.

SKÍATHOS TOWN (CHÓRA)
Built in 1830, with pretty red-tiled houses and a church bell-tower, the village looks almost more Italian than Greek. It stands on a pretty double bay which forms two harbours, one for yachts and one for fishing boats. The bay is lined with smart cafés and restaurants, while offshore, the waters are dotted with pine-covered rocks and islets.

Bourtzi
In the middle of the bay, a small Venetian-built castle guards the harbour. *Closed.*

Moussío Papadiamantis (Papadiamantis Museum)
Here in his former home, a small collection of memorabilia commemorates the island's most famous son, novelist and poet Alexandros Papadiamantis (1851–1911).
Town centre (signposted). Open: weekdays 8.30am–2pm and 5–8pm.

Skópelos Town rises like an amphitheatre above its harbour

SKÓPELOS

A long, thin island with a spine of hills covered in fragrant pine woods, Skópelos is dotted with dozens of tiny chapels tucked away in the woods or perched on steep hillsides: there are more than 100 little churches in its main village alone, and there are up to a dozen convents and monasteries – most of then deserted – scattered around the island.

Steep cliffs give Skópelos striking coastal scenery but make it less appealing to the beach lovers who flock to nearby Skíathos. Instead of kilometres of sand, Skópelos has an array of delicious white-pebble coves, most of them accessible only with difficulty by land, and more easily reached by boat.

Tourism is growing fast, mainly as a result of overspill from nearby Skíathos, whose international airport brings Skópelos too within easy reach. But the island retains its own charm, with small farms growing fruit, olives and nut trees among the ubiquitous pine forest.
6km east of Skíathos.

LIMNONARI

An excellent beach of coarse white sand surrounded by pines. The chirping of cicadas in summer is deafening.
9km southwest of Skópelos Town.

LOUTRÁKI

Ferries from neighbouring islands call at this northern port as well as at Chóra (see opposite). Apart from its narrow, (mediocre) beach, Loutráki has little to offer.
28km northwest of Skópelos Town.

MILIA

By far the biggest and best beach on the island, Milia is a 1.5km curve of small white pebbles backed by steep pine-clad

slopes. So far it remains pleasantly
unspoilt.
14km west of Skópelos Town, on west coast.

SKÓPELOS TOWN (CHÓRA)
The town's typical tall houses rise in tiers
above a deep, narrow bay surrounded by
pine-wooded mountains. With steeply-
pitched stone roofs and jutting balconies
of carved wood and wrought iron, these
dignified dwellings are quite different from
the cosy red-tiled villas of neighbouring
Skíathos or the white cubes of Skýros.
Skópelos is full of character. Pleasant
tavernas and cafés under green shady
trees line the seaside promenade
where generations of islanders stroll at
sundown.

Kástro (Castle)
A coat of whitewash makes the tiny,
ruined Venetian castle less militaristic
than most such island strongholds. There
is not much to see inside, but the view
over the bay, to the three hillside
monasteries opposite, makes the steep
walk worthwhile, especially at sunset.

Moní Evangelistrías (Convent of the Evangelist)
This four-columned church, built in
1712, is famed for its superb Byzantine
icon of the Panagía (Virgin).
*Open: 8am–1pm and 4–7pm. Free
admission.*

Moní Metamórphosis (Monastery of the Transformation)
Illuminated manuscripts, dating from the
post-Byzantine era, are the proudest
possession of this 16th-century
monastery, recently restored to its original
splendour.
*Open: 8am–1pm and 5–8pm. Free
admission.*

Moní Prodrómou (Convent of John the Baptist)
Built in 1721, this monastery features a
carved iconostasis and icons and is
strikingly located with views of the town.
*Open: 8am–1pm and 5–8pm. Free
admission.*

STÁFYLOS
The island's prettiest beach is at the foot
of a natural amphitheatre of cliffs and
steep pine slopes which are dotted with
summer tavernas and small hotels. As it is
close to Chóra, it is therefore also the
most crowded beaches and is lined with
colourful umbrellas and loungers in July
and August.
6km south of Skópelos Town.

VELANIO
To get away from the Stáfylos crowds
(see above), take a 10-minute walk east
along the shore to the neighbouring beach
of Velanio, almost equally attractive but
not yet a full-scale resort strip.

Skópelos Town's churches offer a fine view
across the bay

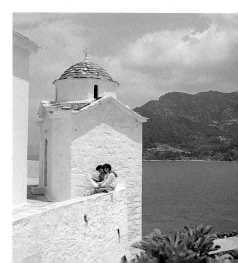

SKÝROS

Lonely Skýros is the joker in the Sporadic pack. Off to the south and east of its companions, it is an hourglass-shaped island of two faces. North of its narrow waist, its pretty main village looks over empty seaward horizons, pine woods and farmlands fringed with long shingle beaches. The southern half of the island is strikingly different, a jagged lunar landscape of shattered boulders where even the goats have a tough time finding greenery.

Skýros is one of the few islands where some older people still wear distinctive traditional costume (see page 144), and it maintains a strong handicrafts heritage which includes beaten-copper dishes and bowls, decorated ceramics, embroidery and elaborately carved wooden furniture. Village homes open straight on to the street, and a walk through the breathtakingly steep lanes of the island's main village allows glimpses into houseproud parlours, decorated and furnished with local products.

Unique to Skýros is a vanishing breed of miniature pony, native since at least the 8th century BC. Once used in the fields, the ponies have been left to fend for themselves with the advent of farm machinery and their numbers have plummeted to around 200.
24km northeast of Kými on Évvoia.

LINARIÁ

The island port offers some accommodation and has a small beach just north of the harbour.
10km south of Skýros Town.

SKÝROS TOWN (CHÓRA)

The island's main village is by far the prettiest of the Sporádes' capitals. A jumble of flat-roofed houses, beneath a dark crag crowned by a fortified monastery, and the ruins of a thousand-year-old Byzantine fastness, make up this idyllic old-fashioned community. Most summer visitors are Greek, so flashy cocktail bars have not yet driven out authentic traditional tavernas and cafés, and off the narrow, car-free main street the town's vertical maze of lanes and alleys is an unchanged puzzle. Visitors wander upwards, downwards and sideways before emerging triumphant at the castle gates.
On the east coast, close to the 'waist' of the island.

Ágios Geórgios
Founded in the 10th century and rebuilt in 1680, this monastery has remarkable frescos of Christ Pantokrator.
Immediately below the castle, entered by an arched gateway below the ramparts. Open: daily 8am–1pm and 5–8pm. Admission free.

Ayía Triáda
The fading glow of this tiny chapel's frescos should not be missed.
50m below the castle. Open: daily. Admission free.

Brooke Memorial
A bronze statue of a youth symbolising immortal poetry commemorates the English poet Rupert Brooke (1887–1915), buried on Skýros after his death (of typhus) aboard a naval hospital ship at Moudros. A male nude, it shocked villagers, and when it was first unveiled they draped it in sheets.
Signposted from the main street.

Kástro
The age-old Byzantine castle offers fine sunset views over the western hills.

At the highest point of the village, entry via the Ágios Geórgios monastery gateway. Open: daylight hours. Free admission.

Magasia

This long, east-facing beach of coarse sand, within sight of Skýros Town, is reckoned to be the best on the island.
1km northeast of Skýros Town.

Moussío Faltaits

A small folklore museum with an excellent collection of traditional weaving, carving, pottery and metalwork.
Opposite the statue of Rupert Brooke

The jumble of flat-roofed houses of Skýros Town: local ceramics and embroideries decorate the parlour of a typical home

(signposted from the village centre) (tel: 0222 91950 or 91232). Open: daily 10am–1pm and 5.30–8pm. Admission charge.

TREIS BOUKES (RUPERT BROOKE'S GRAVE)

The English war poet is buried in an isolated olive grove on the rocky slopes of southern Skýros.
Overlooking Treis Boukes Bay, 23km southeast of Linariá; access by boat from Linariá.

Traditional Costume

In tiny folk museums around the islands you can see the elaborate, colourful costumes of yesteryear: full skirts, embroidered blouses and slippers for women; loose trousers, knee-boots and full-sleeved shirts with gold-braid velvet waistcoats for men. Each island has its own special costume and on more populous islands, like Lésvos, each village had (or still has) its distinctive dress.

The most lavish outfits are for special occasions – wedding feasts or religious festivals – but there are distinctive workaday clothes too, like the huge baggy white cotton shirts and trousers, linen waistcoats and enormous straw sombreros worn by farmers in the Cyclades as recently as 100 years ago.

Sadly, these costumes have all but died out and only vestiges remain. In the wild west of Lésvos, donkey-riding hill farmers still wrap yellow bandanas around their heads, pirate-style, and village women on Chíos favour old-fashioned, snood-like headscarves.

Today there are just three islands where traditional costume is still worn daily, usually by older men and women.

The magnificent, all-black costume of Cretan mountain men is famous, and their knee-length boots, voluminous black pants, shirt and silk headscarf are still to be admired in the remoter villages of southwest Crete.

On Skýros, a few 'good old boys' wear fantastically pleated indigo-dyed trousers, soft pillbox caps, loose collarless shirts and tube-like sandals.

In the village of Ólympoi on Kárpathos (see pages 88–9), it's the women who keep up traditional appearances, wearing an everyday costume of a long skirt with embroidered bodice and headscarf, while a fancier version comes out for special occasions.

Elsewhere, traditional wear has died out. Men and women alike have adopted western European dress long ago, and the only traditional peasant clothing you will see will be from Nepal, Bali or Guatemala – on the trendy backs of visiting backpackers.

Costumes like these are rarely seen except on festival days

GETTING AWAY FROM IT ALL

'The sea was sapphire coloured, and the sky
Burned like a heated opal through the air.
We hoisted sail; the wind was blowing fair
For the blue lands that to the eastward lie.'

OSCAR WILDE,
(1854–1900), *Impression du Voyage*

Getting Away From it All

Greece's most popular islands are of course those which are easiest to get to by air or by direct sea routes which don't involve hours afloat. But there are hundreds more islands, some inhabited by only a few fisher families, others completely deserted, waiting to be discovered. Some may have to wait for a while: infrequent (or non-existent) ferries are a powerful tourism deterrent.

There is no better way to visit these out-of-the-way isles than aboard your own vessel. Take a chartered yacht with an expert crew, and sail in the pampered style of a luxury cruise ship, or jump aboard an old-fashioned island trader converted for island-hopping in comfort.

CAÏQUE CRUISES

The smaller islands and inaccessible beaches of the Dodecanese group (see pages 84–5 and 150–3) can be visited on one of the graceful wooden vessels called caïques which until the coming of steam monopolised inter-island trade. Several of these traditional 25m-long motor-sailers have been converted to carry up to 16 passengers in twin-berth cabins with en-suite hot-water shower and WC. They usually have a crew of four – captain, engineer, steward-deckhand and cook – and as the price of a one-week cruise includes most meals and drinks they are very good value for money, costing little more than a one-week package holiday.

Most cruises operate out of Kós or Rhodes and visit islands between the two. Some cruises also operate north of Kós to Pátmos and the archipelago of sleepy little islands nearby.

Summer only: most companies operate from mid-May to early October. A list of tour operators offering caïque cruises is available from the Greek National Tourist Office (see Directory, page 189).

ISLAND CRUISES

Numerous luxury cruise lines operate itineraries from Píreas (the port of Athens). The most popular destinations are much-photographed Mýkonos (see pages 60–1), Pátmos (see pages 98–9), Rhodes (see pages 102–7) and Thíra (Santoríni) (see pages 66–7). Itineraries can also include ports of call on the Greek mainland and in Turkey.

Cruises can be as short as one day (2–3 weeks is common) and can be arranged through local travel agencies or major hotels.

Allónnios: craft of all sorts ply the blue seas of the Greek islands

Dolphin Hellas Cruises, Akti Miaouli 71, 185 37 Píreas (tel: 01 4512 109).
Epirotiki Lines, Akti Miaouli 87, 185 38 Píreas (tel: 01 4291 000).
Sun Line, Iassonos 3, 185 37 Píreas (tel: 01 4523 417).

FLOTILLA SAILING

For less confident sailors, yacht flotillas, with a lead yacht skippered and crewed by professionals, are the ideal way to explore Greek waters for the first time. Flotillas of up to a dozen fully-equipped modern yachts sail from several islands. The Ionian islands (see pages 24–45), with their sheltered waters, plentiful anchorages and steady breezes, are the most popular archipelago for flotilla sailing.

A list of flotilla sailing specialists is available from the Greek National Tourist Office (see page 189).

YACHT CHARTER

Steady winds, sunny weather and literally thousands of island anchorages make Greece a delight for yacht sailors. There are dozens of yacht charter companies in Greece, based not only in Píreas but at marinas throughout the islands. Rhodes is among the most popular bases for yacht charterers. The government has grandiose plans for a network of new marinas at varios mainland and island ports.

The weather is suitable for sailing from April to October, though strong winds can occasionally keep boats in harbour for days at a time in the Cyclades (the most popular yachting area) in August. Crewed and bareboat charters are available.

A full list of yacht charter companies is available from the Greek National Tourist Office (see Directory, page 189).

ISLAND FLOWERS

Rocky island slopes look barren in high summer, but in spring and early summer they can be a kaleidoscope of red, yellow and purple wild flowers. A hillside which in August is a near-monochrome canvas of grey and tan will be vividly splashed with colour in March or April.

The best time to see the islands in bloom is in the spring, which comes as early as March in southern Crete or as late as May to early June in the northeast Aegean isles. On most islands, much land is useful only for goat pasture, and wild flowers are left to flourish without interference – except from the goats. Island farming is piecemeal, with tiny terraced fields growing varied crops instead of the prairie-style monoculture of northern Europe. More than 6,000 species of flowering plants and ferns grow in Greece, far more than in any other European country, and 750 of them are unique to Greece.

Small fields and meadows lie fallow much of the year, and wild flowers thrive in fields and olive groves alongside cultivated plants.

Poppies, vetches and a dozen kinds of wild daisy are among the most abundant blooms, with anemones, cyclamen, asphodel and crocuses blooming in spring and autumn on slopes and in fields.

Throughout the dry summers, stream-beds are marked by serpentine lines of pink-flowered oleander bushes, whose poisonous leaves deter ever-hungry goats.

The greenish-yellow flowers of fennel (anise) are also summer survivors, seen everywhere in fields and roadsides and harvested to give ouzo, the Greek national drink, its distinctive aniseed flavour. Giant fennel, found on stony pastureland, can reach 4m in height.

Island villages are always a blaze of flowers. Not all homes have the luxury of a garden, but all are adorned with fountains of red geraniums and bright green basil growing in recycled olive oil cans. Vines, purple morning glories and scarlet bougainvillaea (both imports from South America) make shady arbours, and the violet-flowered derris creeper from Australia is another colourful import.

Left: prickly pears grow beside geraniums on a village terrace; above and right: wild flowers make a dazzling display in the short island spring

THE SMALLER ISLANDS

Scattered among the bigger, better-known islands are many tinier isles, some with thriving villages, some deserted but for a handful of fishermen. These dots on the map are not always remote in terms of distance. Many are within an hour's sailing of popular resorts and international airports. But reaching them can be a challenge and it is surprising how crowded some of them can be in high season. Most have one village and a single small beach, and space can be limited in July and August.

Outside the peak months, though, the small isles are a delight for real island fans. If you can be content with a beach, a book, and a simple dinner in an unsophisticated taverna, they offer a sense of peace and isolation – the Greeks call it *isikhia* – that the developed resorts cannot match. And their people, for whom visitors are still something of a novelty, are among the friendliest in Greece.

AGATHÓNISI, ARKOÍ AND LEIPSOÍ

These three islands, with scores of uninhabited rocks and skerries, form a lovely mini-archipelago in the northern Dodecanese, sheltered from northern winds by Sámos and an arm of the Turkish coast.

Agathónisi

A long, low, barren isle of fishermen and goatherds, its name means 'thorny island'. Around 150 people live here and the main village, sheltered among low hills, is simply called Megalo Khorió – 'the big village' – to distinguish it from the even tinier Mikro Khorió.
30km east of Pátmos. Weekly ferries from Pátmos and Sámos (Pythagóreio).

Arkoí

Arkoí, with a population of fewer than 70, is in the midst of a jumble of even tinier rocks, and on a clear day, with the hills of Pátmos, Ikaría, Sámos, Turkey and the smaller islands near by ringing the horizon, it seems to be afloat on an inland lake instead of in the open sea. Its attractions are superbly clear water, excellent snorkelling, and lots of offshore islets on which to sunbathe and picnic.
10km east of Pátmos. Weekly ferries from Pátmos and Sámos (Pythagóreio).

Leipsoí

Almost 600 people live on Leipsoí, making it the metropolis of this mini-island group. Half a dozen tiny white churches, each with its distinctive blue dome, stand out against the hillside terraces which make the most of each patch of fertile land. The broad harbour is home to a small fishing fleet and with its shallow, glass-clear water, it is a natural aquarium full of colourful fish and other Aegean sea life. A sandy beach, five-minutes' walk north of the harbour, is complemented by brilliant white sand coves along the north shore of the island.
8km east of Pátmos; weekly ferries and frequent excursion boats (summer only).

ÁGIOS EFSTRÁTIOS

One of Greece's genuinely remote islands, Ágios Efstrátios lies almost exactly in the centre of the northeast Aegean. Empty horizons on all sides add to the sense of isolation. Its sole village was built to rehouse islanders after an earthquake in 1967 and owners of its identical houses have gradually added individual touches: flowers, vine-arbours and other features. The harbour is so small that large ferries cannot dock and passengers are taken ashore by dinghy.

Leipsoí's hillsides are dotted with tiny blue-domed churches

There are small swimming coves on the east coast.

40km south of Límnos, served by ferries between Límnos and Rafína on the mainland.

ANÁFI

Saucepan-shaped Anáfi has steep sea-cliffs, a high and arid hinterland, around 300 inhabitants and no cars. Almost all the islanders live in the small port of Ágios Nikólaos, on the south coast, or in Chóra, on the hill immediately above it. Anáfi's beach is at Klisidhi, on the south coast, half an hour's walk from Ágios Nikólaos.

1 hour east of Santoríni; infrequent ferries.

CHÁLKI (KHALKI)

Like its neighbours Sými and Tílos (see page 154), Khalki belongs to the southern Dodecanese, is within easy range of Rhodes with its big resorts and international airport, and has become a resort island in its own right. Its harbour village, Emporeió, is very pretty, ringed by fine old houses with peeling stucco façades and drooping balconies. Some of these delightful three-storey mansions are being restored as guesthouses, but many are tumbledown. There is a tree-lined esplanade – far grander than the tiny port seems to need – and several fine uncrowded beaches near by.

50km from Rhodes; daily ferries (from Kámeiros Skála), frequent hydrofoils (from Rhodes Town).

Khorio

Chálki's medieval village is now a ghost-town with a dilapidated watchtower of the Knights of St John on a crag above. The walk from Emporeió is rewarded by a fine view of the east coast of Rhodes (see pages 104–5).

3km west of Emporeió.

Megísti, furthest flung of the Greek islands, lies within a stone's throw of the Turkish hills

FOÚRNOI

This barren, hilly island with its scalloped coastline is named after the old-fashioned outdoor bread-ovens (*foúrni*) still used in a few villages, which its twin hills resemble from a distance. Its small, peaceful harbour village is spectacularly sited on a glorious west-facing bay and there are sandy swimming coves, reached by donkey-tracks, around its coasts.

18km east of Ikaría, served by frequent Píreas-Ikaría-Sámos ferries.

KASTELLÓRIZON (MEGÍSTI)

Greece's most remote island is within a few hundred metres of the Turkish coast. In the 19th century it was an important trading port, but went into a decline after its seizure by Italy in 1912. Before World War II its harbour was a stop on Italian and French flying-boat routes to the Middle East. The war completed the island's decline: from 16,000 people a century ago to 200 islanders now. Despite its ghost-town atmosphere and lack of beaches, it's a delightful island, people seeking it each year it is an increasingly scarce commodity. The population of the only village is less than 100 and facilities for visitors are very primitive.

60km east of Náxos Town; infrequent ferries.

Irákleia

The biggest of the Koufonísi offers a choice of places to swim, a harbour-village set on a scenic, fiord-like bay, and walks over rough hillsides to Panagía, its deserted medieval Chóra.

25km south of Náxos Town; daily ferries.

Koufonísi

Most popular of the group because of the long sandy beach at Finikas, Ano Koufonísia boasts a thriving small fishing fleet berthed in the best natural harbour of the group. There are spectacular sunsets over the bay and the mountains of Náxos.

35km southeast of Náxos Town; daily ferries in summer.

Schoinoússa

Like Donoússa, Schoinoússa is for those in search of peace and quiet, and as on Donoússa more arrive each year overstretching the island's ability to cater to them.

30km southeast of Náxos Town; daily ferries.

with fantastic snorkelling around its rocky shores.

105km east of Rhodes; infrequent ferries and infrequent flights from Rhodes.

KOUFONÍSI

The Koufonísi are four inhabited islands, surrounded by several more deserted isles, lying south of Náxos.

Donoússa

Solitude is the only real attraction of this near-deserted island, and with more

PSARÁ

Rocky, eerie Psará has a special place in the hearts of Greeks. During the War of Independence, this tiny northeast Aegean isle added its fleet of armed merchant ships to the rebel Greek fleet. In 1824, the Turks landed and massacred most of its inhabitants. Psará, which had 30,000 people in its heyday, now has only 460. There is a choice of beaches, with solitude guaranteed.

56km west of Chíos Town. Infrequent ferries.

SÝMI

Tiny Sými retains its delightful serenity despite a daily invasion of excursionists from Rhodes who do little more than eat lunch at a quayside restaurant. In the evening, the island reverts to its natural calm.

27km northwest of Rhodes Town.

Moní Panormítis (Panormítis Monastery)

The 18th-century monastery has a striking carved icon in its small chapel and a mock-baroque campanile dating from 1905.

15km south of Yialos. Open: daily 8am–1pm and 5–8pm. Donation requested.

Pédion

Pédion is situated on a horsehoe-shaped bay with a sand bottom and warm water. It is popular with yachts, and its pebbly, tree-lined beach is upgraded each summer by importing truckloads of sand.

2km east of Yialos on the north coast.

Yialos

Yialos is a ghost town with a pleasant air of faded elegance. Around its deep harbour are ranks of tall, elegantly proportioned neo-classical mansions. Most are mere shells, but many are now being restored, as are the row of windmills which stand above the harbour. Boatbuilding still goes on at the small yard on the bay.

North coast of Sými.

TÍLOS

Blessed with plentiful springs, Tílos abounds with small, fertile valleys and patches of farmland which relieve the barren scenery of its hills.

65km west of Rhodes Town.

Livádia

The island's main village is a pleasant settlement, half-hidden by greenery. On a wide, hill-girt bay, it has a long, pebbly beach.

East coast of Tílos.

Megalo Khorió

This hilltop village overlooks a patchwork of green cultivation. A battlemented fortress of the Knights of St John lends historic interest. Satellite watchtowers of this fortress are scattered

Sponges sold by island sea-dogs are a
popular souvenir of trips to Sými

somewhat incongruously on look-out
hills around the island.
*7km northwest of Livádia. Fortress and
watchtowers freely accessible.*

Mikro Khorió
Deserted since the 1950s,
this ghost village makes a
fine destination for a lovely
walk from Livádia, with
rewarding views from its castle
keep.
*2km west of Livádia. Castle freely
accessible.*

Dolphins and Seals

The appeal of dolphins stretches back hundreds of years, as this fresco at Knosós, Crete, shows

the nets of larger fishing vessels in Turkish waters.

Even more at risk is the Mediterranean monk seal (*Monachus monachus*), now down to 400 individuals living and breeding in seacaves on remote islets in the northern Sporádes, the Ionian, Cyclades and Dodecanese. Growing up to 3m long, it feeds on fish, octopus and squid. Sensitive and shy, it gives birth, usually to only one pup, every one or two years.

Intensive fishing has reduced the monk seal's food supply and oil spills and other forms of pollution also harm them. Rubbish in the water is a growing problem for seals and all other Aegean sea-life, and tourism is largely to blame. Tourism is to blame, too, for rapid development and disturbance of remote coastal zones.

There is something special about dolphins. In ancient times, they were sacred to the god Apollo, and often appear in frescos and on pottery. Today, Greek islanders, like most practical-minded farming people, are not great animal-lovers, but when dolphins are spotted from the deck of an island ferry everybody rushes to look. In fact one of the highlights of any Greek sea journey is the chance of spotting a school of dolphins in the distance or, even better, playing around the ship. The effortless ease with which even young dolphins outpace fast modern ferries is astonishing.

You are most likely to spot dolphins on calm days, when their distinctive curved dorsal fins can be seen lazily breaking the surface a long way off. Sadly, like all Mediterranean sealife, dolphin numbers are dwindling. Heavy pollution from mainland cities – not only in Greece but in Turkey and the Middle East – threatens their environment and they are also often accidentally taken in

How to help

1 Don't chase or approach seals if you see them. Don't go on excursions into sea caves where you will disturb them.

2 Discuss your concern about the survival of the monk seal with fishermen and other local people.

3 Report any illegal activities at sea – such as dynamite fishing, spear-fishing with SCUBA gear, or spear-fishing at night – to port authorities.

DIRECTORY

'Fill high the bowl with Samian wine.'
GEORGE GORDON, LORD BYRON
(1788–1824), *Don Juan*

Shopping

*T*here are bargains to be found, though perhaps not where you would expect. Souvenir shops in resorts from Corfu to Rhodes sell much the same range of slogan T-shirts and brightly coloured imported leisurewear. For more authentic mementoes of your trip, look in the *laiki* – the municipal street market in larger island villages and towns – for items such as brass goat bells, shepherds' wooden walking sticks, or tiny Greek coffee cups.

Contrary to popular tourist belief, haggling over prices is not the norm, though the price of everything does drop outside peak tourist season.

Shops traditionally open between 8am and 1pm, close until around 5pm then reopen until about 8pm, though in major resorts many shops catering to tourists stay open all afternoon and late into the night. Most shops, except those in resort areas, close on Sunday.

Antiquities and imitations

You need an export permit to take real antiques or icons out of Greece. This is rarely granted, and genuine antiquities are in any case very scarce. Beware of fakes. Major archaeological museums in Greece licence a range of accurate and attractive replicas, for example of the enigmatic statues of the Cycladic civilisation, and these are a much better buy.

Beads and bangles

Brightly coloured ceramic beads, necklaces, gold- and silver-plated bracelets and the black and blue glass beads traditionally believed to ward off evil, make cheap and cheerful gifts. Komboloi or 'worry-beads', carried by many island men, are sold very cheaply at street kiosks and in souvenir shops.

Clothing

Good buys include cotton-knit sweaters and on more fashionable islands like Mýkonos, Thíra (Santoríni) or Páros a wide range of attractive and imaginative summerwear by young Greek designers. Cotton and linen prints, silks and cotton knits are popular.

Footwear

Boots and shoes are well-made and affordable. In markets on Crete you will find old-fashioned cobblers selling Cretan riding boots. Sandals sold in tourist markets rarely wear well, but on

Replica statues make good souvenirs

Lace, embroidery and striped woollen blankets are good buys on Crete

Skýros you can buy the unique, hard-wearing sandals worn by islanders which are soled with slices of old car tyre. Main street stores in Rhodes Town are a good bet for classic leather shoes at prices well below the European average.

Jewellery

Jewellers abound in small island towns as well as in big resorts. Traditional designs include a variety of good-luck charms, while on Mýkonos, Páros, Náxos, Thíra (Santoríni) and other islands you will find craftsmen working to modern interpretations and to ancient designs. Silver jewellery is cheaper than average but gold can be more expensive than elsewhere in Europe.

Lace and embroidery

Traditionally made lace napkins and tablecloths are excellent buys in Corfu Town and in Rhodes, but beware of cheap machine-made imitations.

Leather goods

Leather handbags, satchels and travel bags made solely for the tourist market are sold in island markets wherever holidaymakers go. Prices are low, and this is one area where you may haggle. Workmanship is not always first-rate. Examine seams, straps and buckles before buying.

Tax-free shopping

Value added tax at 18 per cent is charged on anything you buy. Tax-free shopping is available to visitors from outside the

European Union at selected shops in the most popular holiday isles. A full list of shops offering VAT refunds to non-EU residents is available from: Tax Free Club, Customer Service Office, Nikis 10, 105 63 Athens (tel: 01 3225 569 or 01 3240 802). The Hellenic Duty Free Shops chain operates duty-free shops for passsengers leaving Greece from airports at Chaniá, Corfu, Irakleío, Kós, Mýkonos, Rhodes, Sámos, Santoríni, Skíathos and Zákynthos.

Mýkanos is famed for its up-market jewellery

Markets

*T*he local *laiki* market in large island towns sells produce, hardware and everyday goods, and with piles of vivid fruit and vegetables it offers lots of photo opportunities and an insight into local lifestyles as well as a chance to buy quirky mementoes of your trip.

The *laiki* takes place weekday mornings and is a great place to stock up on fresh fruit, cheeses and vegetables for picnics or for self-catering. Here too you'll find longer-lasting island specialities like dried and candied fruit, nuts, sunflower and pumpkin seeds, island honey and aromatic herbs. Hours vary seasonally: ask for exact local times at the *dhimotikon* (Town Hall), or island tourist office, or at your hotel.

More formal shopping is patchy and depends very much on the island's holiday clientele: fashionable islands like Mýkonos have designer boutiques and jewellers to compare with the best in Europe; smaller, simpler islands have smaller, simpler shops.

The best island markets for shopping and picture-taking are listed here, together with a sample of other shops.

CORFU

Jewellery in silver and in 18- and 20–22-carat gold can be found in a row of quality jewellers along the Liston arcades behind the Spianada (see pages 28–9). A fine choice of island handicrafts is on sale at the National Welfare Organisation shop in The Village, the reconstructed traditional village 8km northwest of Corfu Town.

CRETE
Irakleío

Crete's capital has a fine produce market on Odós 1866. Look for great bundles of oregano and sage, strings of garlic, and the unique corkscrew-like walking sticks made of Cretan dwarf elm, favoured by island shepherds.

Chaniá

Chaniá's market area spreads throughout the old quarter, east of Odós Halidhon, and is a mix of local merchants and shops catering to visitors too. This is a good place to shop for Cretan boots and well-made leather bags and satchels.

Réthymno

The market stalls and shops which spill out on to the streets around Porta Guora and Odós Ethnikis Antistasis are always colourful and lively. Look for ethnic souvenirs like goat bells or Cretan shepherds' daggers.

CHÍOS
Erytha Gift Shop

Pottery, jewellery and icons inspired by ancient Minoan and Byzantine art. *Hotel Erytha, Karfas, Chíos (tel: 0271 32311).*

LÉSVOS

Odós Ermou, which runs north–south behind the Mytilíni waterfront as far as the castle walls (see pages 118–19), is lined with dusty antique shops selling everything from rusting scimitars and flintlock pistols to tarnished brass and silverware and engravings of island scenes. It's a great street to browse in. In Mólivos, you'll find a number of imaginative souvenir stores.

Fruit and vegetables are piled high in Chaniá's produce market

Platani
Gold and silversmith.
Mólivos (tel: 0253 71356).
Renata Hoffmann
Original hand-painted silks.
Mytilíni 9, Mólivos.

PÁROS
Evangelos Skaramagkas
Finely worked and imaginative gold and silverware.
Kástrou, Paroikia (tel: 0284 22376).

PÁTMOS
Katoi
Authentic Byzantine icons, ceramics and sterling silver jewellery.
Chóra, Pátmos (tel: 0247 31487).

RHODES
Odós Sokrátous, the shopping thoroughfare of the Old Town (see pages 106–7), is packed with fine jewellery and leatherware stores. More jewellers plus excellent shoestores and designer boutiques are to be found on and around Odós Venizelou, in the heart of the New Town. Lambraki, in the New Town, is also a good bet for designer wear.

Babis Ceramics
Original hand-painted ceramics.
Next to Hotel Paradise, Kallithéa, Rhodes (tel: 0241 62906).
Dias
Silks and international designer wear.
Dilberaki 16, Rhodes (tel: 0241 86153).

Louis Feraud Boutique
International designer clothes
Lambraki 39, Rhodes (tel: 0241 35451).
Rodos Gold
Gold jewellery direct from factory.
10km south of Rhodes Town on Líndos road (tel: 0241 65609).
Romani
Designer fashion accessories, Gucci watches and fragrances.
Lambraki 50 (tel: 0241 27451).

SÝMI
Katofli
Ceramics, artworks and icons.
Emporeió, Sými (tel: 0241 71773/72048).

Entertainment

*E*ntertainment in the Greek islands embraces everything from traditional festivals, folk music and dance to modern ballet, experimental theatre and live performances by international artists in every field from Bach and Beethoven to rock-and-roll.

Many islands host month-long summer arts festivals at which the best of Greek artists and international guest performers can be seen and heard and which offer excellent value for money.

Often these take place within the walls of medieval fortresses or on the stages of 2,000-year-old open-air theatres whose acoustics are still as startlingly clear as when they were built.

The daily English-language *Athens News* and the weekly *Greek News*, which are available from news-stands on most resort islands, list upcoming festival and other performances on their events pages.

The Greek National Tourist Office also provides lists of events planned for each year, and information on times, ticket prices and reservations is listed locally by island tourist offices (see page 189)

The free *Summertime* listings magazines published for many islands are another useful source of information on entertainment, nightlife, shopping and other activities (A&P Publishing, Skoufou 10, 105 57 Athens, tel: 01 3226 600).

The Nelly Dimoglou Company of Rhodes keeps traditional dances alive

CINEMAS

A few larger island towns have cinemas, usually old-fashioned and often open-air, where you can catch recently released US and European films with the original soundtrack and Greek subtitles. Posters around town and outside the cinema will tell you what's on and what's on the way.

CULTURAL EVENTS

Annual cultural events on the following islands usually take place in July to September and can include modern and ancient drama, classical and ethnic music and dance.

Itháki
Itháki Music Contest and Theatre Competition
Modern Greek playwrights and composers present their work.
July. Municipality of Itháki (tel: 0674 32795).

Lésvos
Summer programme of drama and Greek musical performances in the medieval castles at Mólivos and Mytilíni.
July to August. Tourist Office for the North Aegean, North Aegean Building, Mytilíni, Lésvos (tel: 0251 42511 or 0251 42513).

Skíathos
Aegean Festival
Festival of music and dance, held for the first time in 1994, featuring Greek and international perfomers.
August to Septembe. Bourtzi Theatre, Skíathos (tel: 0427 23717).

Thásos
Philippi and Thásos Festival
Combined programme of dramatic performances held in the ancient theatre at Limin (see page 126–7)

and at Philippi on the mainland.
July to August. Limin, Thásos (Municipality of Thásos) (tel: 0593 64004 Thásos).

Thíra (Santoríni)
International Thíra (Santoríni) Festival
Festival of music and arts held in a modern venue in the island's picturesque capital.
August to September. Nomicos Convention Centre, Thíra, Santoríni.

DANCING

Luxuries like television, video and hi-fi equipment are relatively new to many islands, and islanders, young and old, have not yet lost the habit of making their own amusement. Dancing is their most exuberant pastime and is a part of any celebration. Even in discos patronised by smart young things from Athens, an evening spent dancing to the latest electronic beat may well end in the small hours with a traditional *sirtos*.

You can sample an evening of the kind of traditional entertainment island Greeks enjoy at any *exoxiko kentro* ('country centre'). These are usually some distance from the town or village, and their clientele is often made up of holidaying Greek expatriates enjoying a nostalgic evening of home cooking, retsina from the wood, powerfully amplified traditional music, and dancing by performers and the audience into the very early hours.

One of the best places to see traditional island dances performed by experts is in Rhodes, where the Nelly Dimoglou troupe of dancers performs outdoors on summer evenings.

Nelly Dimoglou Dance Troupe, Ancient Theatre of Rhodes (tel: 0241 20157). Nightly, May to October.

DISCOS

Tourism has combined with the Greek love of dancing to ensure that every island resort has an oversupply of discos and dance clubs. Even tiny villages may have two or three discos, often in the open air. These start to warm up well after midnight and play an eclectic mix of the latest international dance hits and rock oldies, often staying open until dawn in defiance of a patchily enforced rule that they should close at 2am. Many are no more than a dance floor, bar and sound system overlooking the beach and many survive no more than one or two summers before re-opening under a different guise with a different management and DJ. It is therefore difficult to make hard and fast recommendations, and the venues listed here are just a sampling of what is on offer.

In any case, there is little to choose among island nightspots except for the DJ's taste in tracks. Admission is usually free, but drinks are two to three times as expensive as in an ordinary bar.

Islands with a long-standing reputation for bop-till-you drop nightlife include Corfu, Íos, Páros and Mýkonos, but it is a quiet island indeed that does not have a nightspot and dance venue of some kind.

Amorgós (Eyiali)
Disco The Que.
Órmos Eyialis, Amorgós.
Íos (Chóra)
Íos Club. An exception to the 'fly by night' rule, the Íos Club has been going since the late '60s. Classical music at sunset, dance music till dawn.
Chóra, Íos.
Náxos
Extasis Cocktail Music Bar. *Paralia, Chóra, Náxos.*
Mýkonos
Mýkonos Dance Bar. *North end of Mitropoleos, Chóra, Mýkonos.*
Scandinavia Bar. *Mitropoleos, Chóra, Mýkonos.*
Páros (Paroikia)
Páros caters to a cosmopolitan clientele with the Downunder Australian Bar, Dubliner Irish Bar and Hard Rock Café, all in the same building, 150m inland from the beach at the south end of the esplanade, Akti Vasileou. The Sodoma Club disco, and Opera Club disco (admission charge) are at the north end of the same street.
Rhodes (Rhodes New Town)
Garage. *13 Iroon Politechniou, New Town, Rhodes.*
La Scala. *2km south of town centre next to Rodós Palace Hotel.*
Obsession. *Panagou Shopping Centre, New Town, Rhodes.*

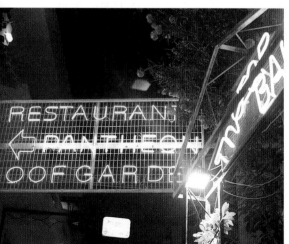

Garish neon points the way to nightlife on Crete

FESTIVALS

Religious festivals in the Greek islands combine solemn ritual with merry-making, feasting, drinking and dancing. The most important events of the island year are also times of family reunion, when sons and daughters who have emigrated return to their island village. Most of the celebrating takes place the night before the holy day itself. Well-behaved visitors are welcome to join in.

Easter

This is celebrated according to the Orthodox calendar throughout Greece with feasting on lamb and goat, usually barbecued outdoors, on Easter Sunday, followed by midnight mass and procession.

Panayiria (Assumption of the Virgin), 15 August

A celebration throughout the islands with feasting and dancing. Special pilgrimages and processions are held at Markopoulo on Kefalloniá, and on Skíathos and on Tínos.

SOUND AND LIGHT

Corfu Town: Palaio Frourio, 15 May–30 September; times and reservations from Corfu tourist office, New Fortress Square (tel: 0661 37520).

Rhodes Town: Palace of the Grand Masters, April to October; times and reservations from Rhodes tourist office,

Dance clubs like Kós's Playboy Club are popular

corner of Arch Makariou and Papagou (tel: 0 241 23655).

TELEVISION AND VIDEO

The television is a fixture in every small island kafeneon or taverna. The national TV channels ET1 and ET2 broadcast a steady diet of imported British and US programmes subtitled in Greek. Satellite TV is spreading fast and is offered by many larger resort hotels. Many hotels and bars in the more popular island resorts also offer a nightly programme of video movies, sports and music programmes from around the world.

Children

*T*he Greek islands and their people welcome children warmly and there are very few places where they cannot be taken. Couples will often be cross-examined: do you have children? If not, why not?

Islanders regard children as an unmixed blessing, and crying babies or the fractious late-night behaviour of tired youngsters will be tolerated in village tavernas and cafés. Above all, life in the Greek islands is lived outdoors almost all year round, and island youngsters are raised on a free-range basis with the whole village and its surroundings as a playground. Visiting toddlers can easily join in.

Food
Food should not be a problem, even if your children are picky eaters who insist on a chips-only diet. These are on every island menu, as are other plain and familiar dishes such as fish and burgers.

Canned soft drinks are universally available, as are most well-known brands of sweets and chocolate bars, ice-cream and ice lollies. Sticky cakes and sweet things from the *zakharoplasteion* (pastry shop) are also a hit with young children.

The seaside
The main attraction for families visiting the islands is the beach, and sea and sand are the focus of most family resorts. Greek seas have virtually no tide, so the sea is always at your doorstep and is usually calm enough even for young children to swim in safety.

Sheltered, gently-shelving sandy beaches suitable for families with small children can be found on many isles.

Things to do
Children with an interest in wild flowers and wildlife will find the Greek islands a delight, with dozens of birds, lizards, tortoises, butterflies and other insects to identify and watch. Those with an interest in marine life will find the clear waters of inlets and harbours as full of sea creatures as any marine aquarium, and will be fascinated by the varied haul unloaded by fishing boats each morning.

Greece welcomes youngsters warmly

Island children spend most of their time outdoors or on the beach

The end of any island pier always attracts a gaggle of junior anglers, and simple hook-and-line kits are sold in all village shops.

Pedaloes, canoes and other simple watersports equipment are for hire at all summer beach resorts, and older children can use them with confidence in shallow waters and enclosed coves. Although island waters have very little tide, they do have strong inshore currents so caution must be used. Bicycles for children and adults can also be rented at some resorts, and donkey-trekking into the hills is offered on several islands including Amorgós, Corfu and Lésvos.

Children with an interest in history will find that ancient sites, medieval castles and deserted fortresses on almost every island offer a fascinating 'hands-on' lesson in the past, and younger children will enjoy scrambling to the highest tiers of the ancient theatres.

In the unlikely event of poor weather, a visit to one of the many island folklore museums with their displays of traditional costumes, kitchenware, tools, weapons and jewellery will keep children entertained.

Purpose-built facilities and entertainment for children are rarely provided in the Greek islands. Many villages have a small playground, though its old-fashioned wood and metal swings and roundabouts and rough gravel are potential hazards for smaller children.

Some larger resorts, hotels and apartment complexes have separate swimming pools for toddlers, and many package tour operators offer 'fun-clubs', child-minding and babysitting services (see Practical Guide, page 181).

Sport

*T*he great sporting passions of Greece are basketball and football, which islanders play enthusiastically on the dusty village pitch and watch avidly on television. Greece's top teams are on the mainland, in Athens and Thessaloníki, but you will see graffiti acclaiming them all over the islands too.

BASKETBALL
Greek Basketball Federation
N Saripolou 11, Athens (tel: 01 8244 125).

SOCCER
Major league matches are played regularly on Sundays at 5.30pm in season (October to April). Tickets are available at each team office.
Greek Soccer Federation, Syngrou 137, Athens (tel: 01 9336 410).

SPORTS FOR VISITORS

GOLF
The Greek islands have an ideal climate for golf, with March to November considered the best months.

Corfu
Corfu Golf Club
18-hole, par-72 course designed by Donald Harradine.
At Ropa, 17km from Corfu Town (tel: 0661 94220).

Rhodes
Afandou Golf Club. *19km from Rhodes Town (tel: 0241 51255).*

TENNIS
Corfu, Crete and Rhodes are the islands best provided with tennis courts. Many major resorts have their own courts. For further information, contact EFOA (Greek Tennis Association), Omirou 8, Athens (tel: 01 3230 412).

TREKKING AND WALKING
The Greek islands are wonderful walking country, offering relatively gentle routes for a day's strolling or much more demanding itineraries lasting one or more days. The Levká Óri (White Mountains) of southwest Crete offer some of the most demanding and rewarding trekking in Europe through

Ideal conditions for windsurfers

Wet, wild fun for all ages

landscapes of savage grandeur. On Samothráki, 1,600m Mount Fengári can be climbed in one full day. Corfu's Pantokrátor region offers gentler walking. Sámos offers trekking in strongly contrasting landscapes, from green woodland to the bare peak of Mount Kerkis, while of the smaller isles, Nísyros, Tílos and Amorgós offer less demanding hikes.

The Greek Alpine Club, which manages refuges in the Cretan mountains, publishes a range of guides and detailed route maps and can advise on mountain equipment and when to go.

Basic mountain safety rules must be obeyed even on shorter walks, especially in the mountains of Crete, as these and many other places are thinly populated and a sprained ankle far from help could spell disaster. Take plenty of water and make sure that someone knows where you are going and when to expect your return. Proper walking boots, not just trainers, are essential for tougher treks. Other essentials include a water bottle and water sterilising tablets.

Ellinikos Oreivatikos Sindhesmos /EOS (Hellenic Alpine Club), Karageorgis Servias 7, Athens (tel: 01 3234 555).

WATERSPORTS FOR VISITORS

SCUBA DIVING

The seas of Greece offer wonderful diving, with excellent visibility. However, because of the risk of theft from underwater archaeological sites, strict rules apply and diving is permitted only in certain areas. Removing or even photographing any antiquities you find is banned, as is spearfishing with scuba gear if close to a beach.

Diving centres in Greece include:

Corfu
Calypso Diving Centre. *Marasli 24, Ágios Gordis, Corfu (tel:0 661 53101).*
Mýkonos
International Diving Club. *Ornos Beach, Mýkonos (tel: 0289 23220).*
Rhodes
Kallithéa Diving School. *PO Box 409, Rhodes (tel: 0241 21690).*

Diving is also permitted off **Paxos** and **Zákynthos**.

WATERSKIING

Waterskiing facilities are available at all holiday beaches in summer and there are waterski schools at most major resorts.

For further information, contact the Greek Waterskiing Association, Stournara 32, Athens (tel: 01 5231 875).

WINDSURFING

Greek island waters, with their reliable breezes, are perfect for windsurfing and boards are for hire at any sizeable resort. A number of international events are held each year.

The west coast of Kós and the bay of Nydrí on Lefkáda are rated among the best windsurfing spots in the Mediterranean.

Food and Drink

WHAT'S ON THE MENU

The best island food is the simplest: fish straight from the boat, vegetables fresh from the field served as salad with wild herbs and olives or in stews. Most resort restaurants offer multilingual menus; where they don't, you will be invited into the kitchen to choose from the pots simmering on the stove. Translations can be puzzling, inviting you to to sample 'smashed bowels in roasted spit' or 'one brain salad'. Puzzling them out is half the fun. Food is very often better in smaller, unsophisticated island villages than in bigger resorts, where pressure of numbers forces restaurateurs to fall back on the freezer and the microwave. In a little family-run pierside taverna off the beaten track the menu will be much more limited, but the fish will be fresher. Few islanders, even in more sophisticated resorts, are trained chefs, and attempts to serve 'international cuisine' are almost always less successful than the basic dishes of the islands.

Only in the smartest restaurants will food be served course by course. *Meze*, a selection of dishes served simultaneously, is a Greek culinary tradition, and in smaller places everything comes at once or in an unexpected order – chips, for example, often arrive as an appetizer.

Islanders, like all Greeks, tend to eat late when they eat out, and a restaurant which seemed empty when you sat down to dinner is often full of diners by the time you are ready to leave.

Fish

Fish is priced according to weight and category. You choose your fish from the kitchen, where it is weighed and the price is calculated before filleting. Seafood is popular but more expensive every year,

Octopus – an island delicacy

Fresh vegetables are preferred to canned or frozen products

with delicacies like *barbounia* (red mullet) and *melanouryia* (blacktail) at the top of the price range. Swordfish (*xikias*) steaks are always available and moderately priced, usually coming in enormous portions. At the cheaper end of the scale are *marides* (whitebait), *goupes* (sprats) and *kalamares* (fried battered baby squid). *Astakos* (langouste, though usually translated as lobster) is expensive by local standards, though most visitors will think it good value. Unfamiliar seafood dishes include *oktapodhi* (octopus), served in a variety of ways, either cold as a snack, grilled, or in a stew (*stifadho*) with rice or pasta.

Meat dishes

Moussaka (lamb or veal cooked in layers of white sauce, cheese and aubergine, or sometimes potato) *yiouvetsi/pastitsio* (beef stewed with noodles in a clay pot), *kotopoulo* (roast or grilled chicken) and *souvlaki* (pork, veal or lamb cooked on a skewer) appear on most menus, as do *kefthedhes* (meat balls in sauce), *paidakia* (lamb chops) or *brisoles* (pork or veal cutlets).

Vegetable dishes

The traditional Greek salad is a meal in itself, and few restaurants will mind if you order it and nothing else. It's basically a great heap of lettuce, tomatoes, onion, cucumber, green peppers and olives, sprinkled with dried herbs. It is known as *horiatiki* ('village salad') only in tourist restaurants, where it is usually served crowned with feta cheese (if you don't want the cheese, ask for *salata horeis feta*, salad without feta).

Dishes like *gemista* (tomatoes or green peppers stuffed with herb-flavoured rice)

Ouzo, Greece's national spirit, comes in many different bottles

and *dolmades* (stuffed vine leaves) may or may not contain meat. Vegetable-only dishes include *vriam* (ratatouille) and a variety of pulses including *fakes* (lentil stew), *gigantes* (stewed broad beans), *mavromati* (boiled black-eye beans served cold with coriander) and *fasolakia* (green beans stewed with tomatoes). Cold dishes include *tsatsiki* (yoghurt flavoured with cucumber and garlic).

Chips are the favoured accompaniment to meat dishes.

If you do not eat meat, try telling the restaurateur that you are a *hortophagos* – a vegetarian.

BEVERAGES

Beer
Almost all beers sold in Greece are strong lagers, brewed locally under licence and always served ice-cold. Common brands include Amstel, Beck's, Henninger, Heineken, Kaiser, and Kronenbourg, all around 5 per cent alcohol by volume and usually sold in 550ml bottles. Imported beers such as Sol and Corona are often sold in smarter bars and British brands

such as Guinness and Newcastle Brown Ale are also found in island resorts with a British clientele.

Prices vary widely and largely depend on where you drink, not what you drink. A small bottle of imported beer in a neon-lit cocktail bar may cost three times as much as a large bottle in a local taverna.

Brandy
Locally made brandy – sometimes described as *koniak* (cognac) – comes in three-, five- and seven-star quality. Sweeter than French brandies, it makes a pleasant after-dinner drink. Best-known brands include Metaxa, Cambas, and Sámos.

Coffee and tea
Kafes elliniko (Greek coffee) comes black and thick, in thimble-sized cups, and is always served with a glass of water. Don't stir it or you will disturb the grounds, which are left in the cup. If you like it without sugar ask for *sketo*; if you like extra sugar ask for *glikou*. Most Greeks drink it *metrio*, with one measure

of sugar. Instant coffee, whatever the brand, is called *Nes* and is often served iced (*frappé*). *Tsai* (tea) is available almost everywhere and is invariably made with Lipton's tea-bags. If you like your tea or coffee with milk, ask for it *me gala*.

Imported and local spirits

Imported liquors such as scotch, bourbon, vodka and gin generally cost a lot more than the local spirits, most of which are destined only to be cocktail ingredients. Measures, however, are always generous.

Ouzo

Sunset is the customary time to take your Greek aperitif, though ouzo is drunk at any hour. A clear, sweet, aniseed-flavoured spirit, it is always served with a glass of water and usually with ice. It turns cloudy when water is added. Ouzo from Lésvos and Chíos is highly thought of.

Retsina

Retsina (a resinated wine) was formerly stored in earthenware jugs proofed with pine resin, which gave it a distinctive flavour. Today, resin is added artificially. It is an acquired taste, but one worth acquiring quickly, as it is by far the cheapest of Greek wines.

In many island villages the taverna will sell retsina *apo to bareli* (from the barrel) and sampling it is always an experience. Whatever you really think, be sure to praise it extravagantly – the landlord may have made it himself!

Soft drinks

All the well-known brands are available on every island, as are various fruit juices sold by the carton. Freshly-squeezed orange juice, available in pricier cafés in resorts, is remarkably expensive in a country which grows so many oranges.

Tsipouro

A clear and lethal spirit made (like Italian *grappa*) from the skins and pulp left over after pressing grapes to make wine. You are unlikely to find tsipouro in most bars: it's a winter drink, kept for local consumption in the coldest months, January and February.

Wine

The Greek islands produce a choice of red, white and dessert wines, all of them affordable and few outstanding. Whites are often better than reds. Sámos produces one of the few Greek wines which will stand international comparison: Samaina, a crisp dry white. The Robola range of red and white wines from Kefalloniá is also highly regarded.

Thíra (Santoríni) produces Vinsanto – strong, sherry-like wines with an alcohol content up to 17 per cent, from grapes grown on its black volcanic soil.

The CAIR and Emery wineries of Rhodes produces a very good sparkling white.

Greek wines are very affordable

RESTAURANTS

You can eat well in even the smallest of island villages, though the menu may be limited to the catch of the day and whatever fruit and vegetables are in season locally. In most resorts and towns there is little to choose between one eating-place and its neighbour, so stroll down the beach or around the harbour and pick whichever takes your fancy.

Eat where islanders or holidaying Athenians eat and you will eat better, cheaper and more varied meals than in restaurants catering only to holidaymakers. For many island restaurants the quality of food is not so important as the setting, the view, the atmosphere or the ebullient charm of the proprietor.

Below we list restaurants on the bigger and more popular islands, as well as a handful of other places which stand out from the crowd.

The following table is an indication of restaurant prices. The D (for drachma) sign indicates the cost of a three-course meal for one without wine. A half-litre carafe of retsina or a bottle of beer costs around DR350, a bottle of red or white wine between DR1,500 and DR2,000.

Very few island restaurants accept telephone reservations (or even have a telephone). Prices are up to 50 per cent higher across the board in international holiday resorts than in backwater island restaurants and may increase their prices by up to 20 per cent a year, so only a rough price guide can be given. Additionally, many restaurants in island resorts are leased by the year: a restaurant may close in October to re-open next spring under different management with a new image and menu, while the previous manager and chef pop up on a different street or even on a different island.

D = up to DR3,000
DD = DR3,000–DR4,500
DDD = DR4,500–DR6,000
DDDD = more than DR6,000

CHÍOS
Perivoli DDD
Excellent local menu, island wines, and Greek dancing every Friday evening. *Argenti 9–11, Kampos, Chíos (tel: 071 31973).*

CORFU
Averof DD
Traditional Greek food, pleasant atmosphere. *Proselendou (old harbour), Corfu Town.*
Danilia Village, Gouvia, Corfu DD–DDD
A choice of international and traditional Greek eating-places on the square of a re-created medieval village. *2km outside Gouvia, 8km northwest of Corfu Town.*

Don't miss fresh island seafood

CRETE
Olympia Garden DD
In a pretty old neo-classical mansion with a leafy outdoor terrace. Good Greek food.
Strategos Koraka 11, Ágios Nikólaos.

Fish restaurants and tavernas
DDD–DDDD
The tiny fishing harbour at the north end of the main esplanade at Réthymno is packed with delightful outdoor fish restaurants. Fine seafood and pleasant atmosphere in all.
Mikrolimano, Réthymno.

KÓS
Most of Kós Town's restaurants and tavernas are along Vasilis Georgiou, the beach esplanade south of the Kástro, or around the harbour on Akti Kountouriouti.

Platanos DD–DDD
Traditional taverna with Greek dishes, beside the castle and the ancient plane tree.
Platía Hippokratous, Kós Town (tel: 0242 28991).

White Tower DD–DDD
Good grill restaurant.
Akti Kountouriouti 13, Kós Town (tel: 0242 22638).

LÉSVOS
Okhtapodhi ('The Octopus')
DD–DDD
The oldest and best of several traditional fishermen's restaurants.
Limenon, Mólivos.

LÍMNOS
Psarotaverna O Glaros DDD
Excellent seafood restaurant with a fine view of the floodlit Genoese castle.
On the small fishing harbour, 500m east of Platía Oktobriou 8

Greek salad is a meal on its own

MÝKONOS
El Greco DDDD
Stylish, with a sophisticated Greek-flavoured menu, up to international standards for once.
Enoplon Dinameon, Tria Pigadhia, Mýkonos Town.

Pelican DDD
On the picturesque waterfront, by the twin cathedrals. Lovely view, good seafood.
Platía Mitropolis, Alefkandhra, Mýkonos Town.

PÁROS
Bellevue DD
Fondue and hot-stone dishes with a view of the bay.
Paralia, 200m south of ferry pier, Páros waterfront.

RHODES
Oasis DD
Friendly, good-value restaurant serving Greek dishes and local wine.
Platía Douleios, corner of Omirou and Fanouriou, Rhodes Old Town.

Hotels and Accommodation

*F*inding somewhere to stay is rarely a problem in the Greek islands in summer. There is accommodation to suit all pockets in all but the tiniest villages, where you may find the local shopkeeper is willing to rent a spare room (or, in summer, a camp bed in the garden or on the roof).

However, almost all island pensions and hotels close in mid-October and do not reopen until April. You should also book well ahead for accommodation at Easter and Panayiria (see page 165) when millions of Greeks return to their islands.

Accommodation is licensed by the government, which classifies hotels, pensions, apartments and privately-rented rooms in categories A to E. Accommodation is rated on services and facilities, not on quality, so a drab old hotel with in-room television and telephone and a mediocre restaurant will rate higher than a bright new one without such services. Many attractive new properties have no grading. The system should be treated with caution.

It does, however, give a guide to prices. In July and August prices can be up to 30 per cent more than in the shoulder-season months. When this book was researched a recently-built twin room with en-suite facilities cost from around DR5,000 in a small family-run pension to DR50,000 in a top hotel. A C-class hotel (equivalent to 3-star) costs between DR10,000 and DR15,000 per room.

APARTMENTS

Self-catering apartments on the most popular islands are excellent value for money, especially for families. Most have two bedrooms (or one bedroom and a convertible lounge) and a kitchen with two-ring electric cooker, fridge, crockery, cutlery and cooking utensils. In high season they are used mainly by package tour companies, but in spring and autumn are often available at bargain rates to independent travellers.

CAMPSITES

Visitors who have enjoyed the generally excellent campsites on the Greek mainland will be disappointed by the poor facilities, dirt, litter and lack of amenities of most island campsites. Mainly used by young backpackers on a tight budget, they are no bargain.

HOTELS

A-class luxury hotels are to be found only on islands which are long-standing favourites, primarily Corfu, Crete (Elounda area) and Rhodes. An exception is the superb Akti Mýrina hotel, a Caribbean-style bungalow complex on the otherwise unexciting island of Límnos (see page 117). Akti Mýrina Hotel, 81400 Límnos (tel: 0254 22681). There are C-class hotels, usually big, bland and busy, on every island with an international airport.

D- and E-class hotels, found in many larger commercial ports, are very cheap but often grubby and run-down. For lone travellers, they offer the advantage of single rooms at lower rates.

PENSIONS

Small, family-run pensions, usually with around a dozen twin-bedded rooms, are excellent value. Most are recently built, with en-suite facilities in rooms and solar-heated water.

UNIQUE PLACES TO STAY

The Greek National Tourist Office's Traditional Settlements are traditional buildings converted into comfortable guesthouses with modern facilities. Rates compare with B- and C-class hotels – worth every drachma for their atmosphere and location in the most beautiful landscapes and villages of the Greek islands. There are Traditional Settlements in Mestá on Chíos (see pages 114–15) (tel: 0271 76319) Psará (see page 153) (tel: 0272 61293), and Oía on Thíra (Santoríni) (see pages 66–7) (tel: 0286 71234).

At Argirónisoss, 3km off the north coast of Évvoia, you can sample the millionaire life on a fully-staffed private island which sleeps up to 12.

VILLAS

Luxury villas, some with their own pool and landscaped grounds, can be found

The islands have a handful of grand old-fashioned hotels

on Corfu, Paxoí and some other islands. Travel agents should have information of those tour operators offering villa packages.

On Business

*D*espite repeated European Union grants and loans, the urgings of the International Monetary Fund, and attempts to modernise and reform, Greece's economy remains the most problematic in the EU.

Business is burdened by an inefficient and underpaid bureaucracy and privatisation of the cumbersome and militant public sector, has been put on hold.

The three-year war in Bosnia and the breaking up of the former Yugoslavia, Greece's northern neighbour, also had a disruptive effect on the economy.

Shipping and tourism compete as Greece's top two foreign currency earners, with agriculture in third place. The shipping industry is in the hands of a relatively small number of private companies, several of which also extend into the tourism sector, but small, family-run operations predominate in farming and tourism.

Many Greek executives are educated in the US, Britain and Canada and almost all speak fluent English and are familiar with the needs of their overseas colleagues. However, a new breed of executive sees Europe, rather than the Anglo-Saxon countries, as its role model, and since joining the European Union Greece's economy has stepped out of the shadow of the US.

ACCOMMODATION

Major hotel chains are thin on the ground in most of the islands, though Hilton International has a property in Corfu. Greece's major home-grown hotel groups, Capsis, Chandris, and Astir, have reliable hotels on the more popular resort islands. Elsewhere, properties are designed primarily for holidaymakers but offer basic business-traveller requirements such as direct dial phone facilities in bedrooms. Fax and telex communications can be found on almost all islands. However, finding international-standard accommodation anywhere except Corfu, Crete and Rhodes outside the April to October holiday season poses problems, as most properties close down for winter.

BUSINESS ETIQUETTE

Greek business etiquette is relaxed. Punctuality is appreciated, but turning up late for a meeting is not a mortal sin. Normal business-wear is jacket and tie for men (a suit is not essential) and skirt, dress or trouser suit for women. Not all offices are air-conditioned, and in summer many executives dispense with jacket and tie in favour of open-necked, short-sleeved shirt and slacks. Shake hands on meeting and parting. Many offices close between midday and 4pm and many business people take an extended holiday in mid-July to late August.

BUSINESS TRANSPORT

To and from the islands Olympic Airways operates an extensive inter-island network connecting islands with each other and mainland gateways, primarily Athens and Thessaloníki. Flights should be reserved before you arrive in Greece as they are often overbooked. Informally, preference is given to passengers connecting with international Olympic flights. There are no direct international scheduled flights to the Greek islands from Britain or the USA. Air taxi and helicopter services are available from Athens airport.

Alternative rapid transport to and between islands is offered in summer by a network of high-speed hydrofoils and catamarans.

On the ground
Taxis are the most convenient way of getting around and meet most island flights and ferries. Car rental is available on virtually all islands through international and local companies but is expensive. Hiring a taxi by the day is a practical alternative.

COMMUNICATIONS
Surprisingly, phoning locally or internationally is often easier on smaller islands than it is in Athens: while the capital struggles with elderly infrastructure quite inadequate to its needs, many islands have newer, more recently installed equipment. Operators are usually helpful and competent in English. Fax facilities are widely available, even in out-of-the-way places and family-run hotels. Sending a fax message is often easier and less time-consuming than making a phone call.

CONFERENCE AND EXHIBITION FACILITIES
Several islands offer facilities for conferences and exhibitions. Corfu upgraded its facilities when it hosted an EU summit in 1994, and is a popular meetings and incentive travel destination, as are Rhodes, Crete and, to a lesser extent, Kós. The best conference and exhibition venues are in major international hotels.

Corfu
Corfu Hilton, Kanoni, Corfu (tel: 0661 36540/9).
Crete
Elounda Beach Hotel, Elounda, Crete (tel: 0841 41412/3).
Kós
Caravia Beach Hotel, Marmári, Kós (tel: 0242 41291/4).
Rhodes
Rodos Palace Hotel, Rhodes (tel: 0241 25222/32).

MEDIA
Two English-language magazines, *Greece's Weekly* and *Odyssey*, are useful sources of information for the business traveller. *Greece's Daily*, a news preview distributed by fax, provides news and analysis ahead of the Greek and international daily press.

SECRETARIAL AND TRANSLATION SERVICES
Bilingual secretarial services and translation facilities are not widely available in island hotels or elsewhere.

Practical Guide

ARRIVING

By air

There are international airports on Corfu, Crete, Kárpathos, Kefailoniá, Kýthira, Kós, Lésvos, Mýkonos, Rhodes, Sámos, Thíra (Santoríni), Skíathos and Zákynthos receiving charter flights between April and November from most European countries. There are no direct scheduled services to the islands from the UK or the USA: all scheduled services use Athens or Thessaloníki airports on the mainland, connected to the above airports by domestic flights, which also serve a steadily expanding network which includes Chíos, Límnos, Léros, Páros, Skýros, Náxos and Kastellórizo.

Domestic flights are often overbooked. If you plan to fly within Greece, book your flights before you leave home and remember to reconfirm. Facilities at island airports are basic. On most islands, taxis are the only transport option for passengers who are not on a package holiday. Car rental companies have desks at most of the larger island airports.

By sea

Many ferry companies ply the Greek island routes, connecting them with each other and with Píreas, the port of Athens. Journey times range from under an hour to islands close to the mainland to around 14 hours (from Píreas to Rhodes). Ferries also operate from Thessaloníki, Kavála and Alexandroúpoli on the northern mainland to the Sporádes and Northeast Aegean isles and from Igoumenítsa and Pátra on the west coast to the Ionian isles. You can also arrive in Greece via Corfu with ferries from the Italian ports of Ancona, Bari, Otranto and Brindisi; via Crete from Egypt and Israel; and via Rhodes, Kós, Sámos, Chíos and Lésvos from ports on the nearby Turkish coast.

Passports and visas

Passports are required by all except

On most islands, buses are timed to meet ferries

European Union citizens, who may use national identity cards. British visitors must carry a full British passport and are permitted a maximum stay of six months. Citizens of the USA, Canada, Australia and New Zealand may enter for up to three months without a visa, but travellers from South Africa do need a visa. Travellers who require visas should obtain them in their own country of residence, as it may prove difficult to obtain them elsewhere.

CAMPING

A list of island campsites is available from the Greek National Tourist Office (see page 189) and from the Greek Camping Association, Solonos 102, 10680 Athens (tel: 01362 1560). Camping or sleeping rough on beaches is illegal, a rule which is widely ignored.

CHILDREN

There are few special facilities for babies or older children, except where provided by package tour companies for their clients. Services provided by holiday companies often include babysitting for younger infants, playgroups for toddlers, and activity groups for younger children. Baby milk, food and nappies for infants are available in tourist resorts at most mini-markets and elsewhere from the *geniko emporion* (general store) or from pharmacies.

CLIMATE

Winters are mild and short, with rainfall at its highest and temperatures at their lowest in February – around 8–10°C, much colder on the mountains of Crete and anywhere above the 1,000m level. By March, days are warmer and April and May offer changeable weather with the likelihood of rain balanced by the possibility of warm sunshine. Rain rarely falls between June and late September. Midsummer temperatures average more than 30°C.

CRIME

Greece's islands have very low rates of theft or violent crime against tourists. That said, normal caution should be exercised. Look after money, travellers' cheques, credit cards and other valuables.

CUSTOMS REGULATIONS

Normal EU rules apply. Non-EU visitors may bring in 200 cigarettes, 50 cigars or 250g of tobacco, one litre of spirits, two litres of wine or liqueurs, 50ml of perfume and 250ml of cologne. It is forbidden to export antiquities and works of art found in Greece.

DRIVING

Accidents

• If possible, set up warning signs. Your hire car should be equipped with a

WEATHER CONVERSION CHART
25.4mm = 1 inch
°F = 1.8 × °C + 32

RÓDOS

October–January
May–September

LÉSVOS

November–January
June–August

ZÁKYNTHOS

November–January
June–August

If you get lost, islanders are
always happy to help

warning triangle, but
not all are.
• If someone is injured,
the accident must be
reported to the police
(see page 184). Passers-
by in such cases are
required to stop and
assist. Contact the
police as a precaution,
even if the only damage is to vehicles.
• If you can, write down the names and
addresses of other drivers involved, the
make and licence plates of vehicles, and
the names of any witnesses. Write down
the date and time of the accident and if
possible take photographs.
• Under no circumstances admit liability,
sign any statement of responsibility, or
lose your temper.

Breakdown

The Automobile and Touring Club of
Greece (ELPA) provides tourist
information and road assistance. Tel:
174 and tel: 104 respectively on all
islands except: Corfu (tel: 0661 39504);
Crete, Irakleío office (tel: 081 289440),
Chaniá office (tel: 0821 26059). ELPA's
coverage of the islands is patchy, but
there are competent vehicle repair shops
and mechanics in most villages.

Car hire

International rental chains are
represented on all resort islands, with
desks in island capitals and at
international airports. Car hire is
available from small local companies on
almost every island. Car hire is expensive
and you may well find it cheaper to hire
through an international chain before

leaving home. Rental cars, even from
major chains, are often under-maintained.
Check tyres, brakes, steering, spare tyre
and lights before leaving the depot (also
see Rules of the road on page 184). Full
collision damage waiver (CDW), personal
accident insurance, bail bond and liability
cover is essential.

Even international companies often
exclude damage to the underside of the
vehicle or the tyres from their CDW
provisions. Make sure your own insurance
covers such damage.

Documentation

A full British or other EU driving licence
is valid. Most other nationalities need an
international driving licence.

Drink-driving

Penalties are severe and the best advice is
to avoid alcohol altogether when driving.

Fines

Police may impose fines for motoring
offences on the spot but may not collect
them. The fine must be paid at a Public
Treasury office or a bank within 10 days.

Fuel

Petrol costs around the European
average. Lead-free fuel is widely

available. It is forbidden to carry fuel in a container in the vehicle. Few petrol stations accept credit cards, and the majority are not self-service. Diesel fuel is considerably cheaper than petrol.

Navigation, maps and road signs
Romanised (ie conventional Western) spellings of Greek place-names vary. However, the differences are generally not so great as to make a name unrecognisable. On main roads, signs are in the Roman alphabet as well as in Greek. On some routes, there will probably be no signs. Beware, too, that many newly-built roads are not shown on island maps.

Rules of the road
Speed limits are 50kph in built-up areas, 80kph outside built-up areas. In practice, much lower speeds than these are advisable on winding and poorly-surfaced island roads.

Seatbelts, where fitted, must be worn. You can be fined for not carrying a warning triangle, fire extinguisher and first aid kit. Many rental cars lack these.

ELECTRICITY
Voltage is 220V AC. You may require an adaptor for the round two-pin sockets used in Greece. Power cuts are not uncommon so take along candles and/or a good torch. Visitors with appliances using US-style 110V power supply need a step-down transformer and socket adaptor.

EMBASSIES AND CONSULATES
Australia
Mesoghion 15, Athens (tel: 7757 650/4).
Canada
Gennadhiou 4, Athens (tel: 7239 510/9).
New Zealand
Semitelou 9, Athens (tel: 7710 112).

United Kingdom
Ploutarchou 1, Athens (tel: 2780 006).
USA
Vassilissis Sofias 91, Athens (tel: 7212 951/9 and 7218 400/1).

EMERGENCY TELEPHONE NUMBERS
Ambulance: 166
General Emergency: 100 (manned by the police and dealing with crime, fire and medical emergencies).

HEALTH
There are no mandatory vaccination requirements and no recommendations other than to keep tetanus and polio vaccinations up to date. Vaccination against hepatitis A and typhoid is also recommended if you intend to travel to some of the remoter areas. AIDS is present. Food and water are safe.

All EU countries have reciprocal arrangements for reclaiming the cost of medical services. UK residents should obtain form E111 from any UK post office. Claiming is a laborious, drawn-out process and you are only covered completely for medical care, not for secondary examinations (such as X-rays), emergency repatriation and so on. You are therefore strongly advised to take out a travel insurance policy to cover all such eventualities. You can buy such insurance through the AA, branches of Thomas Cook and most travel agents.

MEASUREMENTS AND SIZES
Greece uses standard European measurements and sizes (see page 185).

MEDIA
The English-language newspapers *Athens News* (daily) and *Greek News* (weekly) give a quirky insight into national news

and views. The bi-monthly glossy magazine *Odyssey* takes a more thoughtful approach.

British, US and European newspapers are on sale in most resort islands 24 to 48 hours after publication. English news bulletins are broadcast on the ERT2 radio station (98KHz) at 2pm and 9pm. The BBC World Service can be received on 9.41, 12.09 and 15.07 MHz.

MONEY MATTERS

The Greek currency is the drachma (DR). Coin denominations include 20, 50 and 100 drachma, and notes are in 100, 500, 1,000 and 5,000 denominations. Most major currencies, travellers' cheques and Eurocheques can be exchanged at banks, post offices and travel agencies. The latter charge a higher commission but are open when banks and post offices are shut. Banks and post offices generally open 8am–2pm weekdays only, but hours may vary.

Men's Suits

UK	36	38	40	42	44	46	48
Rest of Europe	46	48	50	52	54	56	58
US	36	38	40	42	44	46	48

Dress Sizes

UK	8	10	12	14	16	18
France	36	38	40	42	44	46
Italy	38	40	42	44	46	48
Rest of Europe	34	36	38	40	42	44
US	6	8	10	12	14	16

Men's Shirts

UK	14	14.5	15	15.5	16	16.5	17
Rest of Europe	36	37	38	39/40	41	42	43
US	14	14.5	15	15.5	16	16.5	17

Men's Shoes

UK	7	7.5	8.5	9.5	10.5	11
Rest of Europe	41	42	43	44	45	46
US	8	8.5	9.5	10.5	11.5	12

Women's Shoes

UK	4.5	5	5.5	6	6.5	7
Rest of Europe	38	38	39	39	40	41
US	6	6.5	7	7.5	8	8.5

Conversion Table

FROM	TO	MULTIPLY BY
Inches	Centimetres	2.54
Feet	Metres	0.3048
Yards	Metres	0.9144
Miles	Kilometres	1.6090
Acres	Hectares	0.4047
Gallons	Litres	4.5460
Ounces	Grams	28.35
Pounds	Grams	453.6
Pounds	Kilograms	0.4536
Tons	Tonnes	1.0160

To convert back, for example from centimetres to inches, divide by the number in the third column.

Credit cards are accepted only in larger and more expensive hotels, shops and some restaurants in more popular resorts. MasterCard and Visa are the most widely accepted.

Thomas Cook travellers' cheques free you from the hazards of carrying large amounts of cash and in the event of loss or theft they can quickly be refunded. Sterling cheques are recommended, though cheques in US dollars and major European currencies are accepted. Large hotels, some shops, ticket and travel agencies, and car rental offices in main resort islands accept travellers' cheques in lieu of cash.

The following branches of Thomas Cook can provide emergency assistance in the case of loss or theft of Thomas Cook MasterCard travellers' cheques. They can also provide full foreign exchange facilities and will change currency and cash travellers' cheques (free of commission in the case of Thomas Cook MasterCard travellers' checks).

Karayeorgias Servis 4, Sindagma, Athens.

Thomas Cook Bureau de Change, Othonos Amalias 25, Pátras.

NATIONAL HOLIDAYS

Note that Easter and associated movable feasts are determined by the Greek Orthodox calendar. Dates for Easter can vary from the Christian calendar by up to three weeks.

New Year's Day (1 January)
Epiphany (6 January)
Shrove Monday ('Clean Monday')
Independence Day (25 March)
Good Friday
Easter Sunday
Easter Monday
Labour Day (1 May)

Day of the Holy Spirit
 (Whit Monday)
Assumption of the Virgin Mary
 (15 August)
Ochi Day (28 October)
Christmas Day (25 December)
St Stephen's Day (26 December)

OPENING HOURS

Banks, see Money Matters page 185.

Museums and sites

Opening hours given by official sources often bear no relation to the hours in force, which may change without notice. Most sites are open 8.30am–3pm, Tuesday to Sunday. Some major sites on Crete stay open longer in summer. Winter hours (November to March) are usually shorter than summer (April to October).

Shops

These traditionally open from 8am–1pm and from around 5pm–8pm, but shops catering to tourists usually stay open longer. Most shops outside main resort areas close on Sunday.

ORGANISED TOURS

Organised tours arranged by tour agencies at your resort can be an affordable way of exploring the island if you have no transport of your own or are reluctant to drive. Drawbacks include those of travelling with a group.

PHARMACIES

A green or red cross marks the *farmakio*. Greek chemists have some medical training and can give advice and prescribe medicines for common ailments. Pharmacies open during normal shop hours and are closed on Saturdays and Sundays.

PLACES OF WORSHIP

Sunday services at most Orthodox churches are held from around 7.30am and last for some hours. Decently dressed visitors (long trousers and shirt sleeves for men, below-the-knee and arm-covering dresses for women) may attend. There are Roman Catholic churches on Tínos and Sýros.

POLICE

See Emergency Telephone Numbers.

POSTAL SERVICES

Most larger island villages have a post office, distinguished by its prominent circular yellow sign. They are normally open during shop hours, but city-centre post offices are also open Saturday mornings. It is often quicker to change money at a post office than at a bank. Stamps (*grammatosima*) are also sold at kiosks and postcard shops. Parcels for posting must be inspected by the post office clerk before sealing. Air-mail letters take three to six days to reach the rest of Europe, five to eight days for North America, and slightly longer for Australasia. Cards take much longer.

PUBLIC TRANSPORT
Island buses

Buses are the only public transport available on the Greek islands. Frequencies and services are geared to the needs of islanders, not of tourists: buses are cheap, but hot, are crowded, rickety and do not always serve the sights or beaches you want to go to at the time you want to go, if at all. Double-check

A red or green cross indicates a pharmacy

the destination with the conductor: destination boards often indicate where the bus has come from, not where it is going. Buy tickets on board.

Ferries

Píreas, the port of Athens, is the main gateway to the Aegean islands. Many nearby islands are served by hydrofoils, some of which go, not from the main Píreas harbour, but from Zea Marina, about 3km away. Hydrofoils and ferries also go to Évvoia and to the Cyclades from Rafina, about 30km east of Athens.

Up-to-date timetables are published monthly by the Greek National Tourist Office (see page 189). Many islands are served by ferries from other mainland ports. These include:
Alexandroúpoli (to Thásos, Samothráki)
Astakós (to Itháki, Lefkáda)
Igoumenítsa (to Corfu, Paxoí)

Kavála (to Thásos, Samothráki)
Kyllíni (to Zákynthos, Kefalloniá)
Náfplio (to Cyclades islands)
Pátra (to Corfu, Ionian islands)
Thessaloníki (to northeast Aegean
islands, Sporádes)
Vólos (to Sporádes)
Gýtheio (to Kýthira, Antikýthira, Crete).

Taxis

Taxis are everyday transport for
islanders, and will go virtually anywhere.
Fares are metered and most taxi-drivers
are friendly, honest and helpful though
do take care when going to and from
airports, where overcharging is common.
Beware, too, in Athens and Píreas where
taxi drivers are notoriously dishonest
with tourists.

SENIOR CITIZENS

Older visitors accustomed to cooler
climates may find the islands pleasanter
in April or May, or after mid-September,
when the weather will be warm but not
punishing. Just as Greeks love children,
they also respect older people, but age
has no special privileges. Older people
are expected to fend for themselves, for
example, when boarding a bus or ferry,
and in a country where queueing for public
transport is unknown this can be trying.

TELEPHONES

The easiest way to call is from a metered
telephone in a local tour agency or street
kiosk. Many small hotels and shops also
have metered phones. You pay at the end
of the call. Few of these allow the use of
AT&T or similar charge cards, or reverse-
charge (collect) calls or incoming calls.
Metered phones are also available in
booths at offices of OTE (Greek
Telecommunications Organisation).
You can buy telephone cards for use in
public booths from OTE offices, many
shops and kiosks.
Dialling codes from Greece are:
Australia: 0061
Canada and USA: 001
New Zealand: 0064
UK: 0044
Ireland: 00353
International operator: 161.

In this book, island area codes are
included in all telephone numbers.
Dialling codes within Greece for the
three major cities, all on the
mainland, are:
Athens: 01
Pátra: 061
Thessaloníki: 031

TIME

GMT+2 (+3 in summer).
Clocks change in spring and
autumn on the same date as
other EU countries, but the
time change does not always
coincide with other countries
such as the USA.

Phone home from the OTE office

TIPPING

Service is included in restaurants but it is common to leave small change on the table as an additional tip. This is also widely done in bars and cafés. There is no pressure to tip in hotels but a small tip will be welcomed. In taxis, 'keep the change' is normal practice.

TOILETS

Standards vary enormously but there have been dramatic improvements. Toilets in cafés and tavernas are usually better than public facilities. Greek plumbing is narrow-bore and easily blocked because of low water pressure, so in all places except the latest modern hotels you are asked not to flush toilet paper but to put it in the bin provided.

TOURIST INFORMATION

The Greek National Tourist Office (GNTO) has offices worldwide and provides a range of information which includes hotel listings for all parts of the country, up-to-date transport schedules, and information on sites and events.

Abroad:
Australia
51–7 Pitt Street, Sydney NSW 2000 (tel: 02 241 1663).
Canada
1300 Bay Street, Main Level, Toronto, Ontario M5R 3K8 (tel: 416 968 2220), 1223 Rue de la Montagne, Montreal, Quebec, H3G 1Z2 (tel: 514 871 1535).
United Kingdom
4 Conduit Street, London W1R 0DJ (tel: 0171 734 5997).
USA
645 Fifth Avenue, New York NY 10022 (tel: 12 421 5777).
168 North Michigan Avenue, Chicago IL 60601 (tel: 312 728 1084).

611 West 6th Street, Suite 2198, Los Angeles CA 90017 (tel: 213626 6696).

In Greece:
Corfu
Corfu Tourist Office, New Fortress Square, Corfu (tel: 0661 37520).
Crete
Chaniá Information Office, Kriari 40, 731 00 Chaniá (tel: 0821 26426), Irakleío Tourist Office, Xanthoudidou 1, 712 02 Irakleío (tel: 081 228225).
Kefalloniá
Information Office of Argostóli, Provita Teloniou Customs Office Dock (tel: 0671 22248).
Lésvos
North Aegean Tourist Office, Tz. Aristarchou 6, North Aegean Regional Building, Mytilíni (tel: 0251 42511).
Rhodes
Tourist Office of the Dodecanese, Arch Makariou and Papagou, 851 00 Rhodes (tel: 0241 23655).
Sámos
Sámos Information Office, 25 Martiou 4, 831 00 Sámos (tel: 0273 28582).
Sýros
Ermoúpoli Information Office, Town Hall, Ermoúpoli 841 00 (tel: 0281 22375).

TRAVELLERS WITH DISABILITIES

Facilities for disabled travellers in the Greek islands are poor. Hotel lifts (where available) are often too small for wheelchairs and ramps are extremely rare. Sidewalks, where they exist, are narrow and uneven, and roads often deeply potholed. Most island sites (and sights) are atop steep hills. Before leaving the UK, contact RADAR, 25 Mortimer Street, London W1N 8AB (tel: 0171 637 5400) and the Holiday Care Service (tel: 01293 774535) for general help and advice.

ACKNOWLEDGEMENTS
The Automobile Association wishes to thank the following photographers, libraries and associations for their assistance in the preparation of this book.
MARY EVANS PICTURE LIBRARY 10, 11, 101a
R GAULDIE 19
T HARRIS 2, 32, 33, 36, 37, 38, 39a, 39b, 58, 139, 140, 141, 152/3
NATURE PHOTOGRAPHERS LTD 43a, 43b (J Sutherland)
PICTURES COLOUR LIBRARY LTD 45b, 168
SPECTRUM COLOUR LIBRARY 56, 57, 164/5, 169
ZEFA PICTURES F/Cover

All remaining pictures are held in the Association's own library (AA PHOTO LIBRARY) with contributions from the following photographers:
12, 13, 22, 69, 86, 87, 88/9, 90, 91, 92, 93, 94, 95, 96, 97, 98, 99, 100, 100/1, 101b, 102, 104, 105, 107, 108/9, 108, 111, 130a, 130b, 130/1, 151, 154, 154/5, 155, 162, 167, 171a, 173, 179, 186, 187a, 187b (S L Day); 79, 80, 131, 156 (P Enticknap); Spine, 1, 14, 15, 17, 20, 55, 59, 60, 61, 63, 64, 65, 67a, 67b, 68/9, 70, 71, 72, 75, 77, 149a, 158, 159b, 171b, 175, 177b, 181a, 181b, 183, 188 (T Harris); 133a, 133b, 135a, 135b, 136, 137, 143a, 143b, 144, 147, 157 (R Moore); Inset, 4, 16, 18, 81, 83, 109a, 149b, 159a, 161, 164, 166, 174 (K Paterson); 23, 41a, 41b, 42/3, 45a, 109b, 114, 115, 116, 117, 119, 121, 123a, 123b, 125, 126, 127, 129, 149c, 172 (A Sattin); 5, 24, 26, 27, 28, 29, 30/1, 35a, 35b, 48, 50, 51, 145, 177a (J A Tims); 46/7, 49, 148, 170 (P Wilson)

CONTRIBUTORS
Series adviser: Melissa Shales   **Designer:** Design 23   **Copy editor:** Paul Murphy
Verifier: Judy Sykes   **Indexer:** Marie Lorimer